Venus and I

Venus and I
Anja Schäfer

1st edition

Publisher's Website: *https://discuspublishing.com*

Cover Design & Layout: Anja Schäfer

ISBN: 978-3-910804-02-9 (Print)

ISBN: 978-3-910804-03-6 (Ebook)

Anja Schäfer

Venus and I

My Journey of Coming to Remembrance of my Soul Mission

– 25 years with Omnec Onec –

Table of Contents

Preface

The book you hold here in your hands came about through a stream of consciousness and writing during a two-week trip. After my return, I wrote the last two chapters in Germany. I knew during the trip which chapters were missing and that no more would be added.

You can consider this book as a kind of narrative in diary form, with spiritual and actual information woven into it. It has no claim to completeness and I do not promise to answer all questions that may arise. The style is relatively pure told like story-telling.

This book comes from my heart and not from my head.

May it give you inspiring and also pleasurable reading hours.

Let's connect more and more and create a wonderful new world together!

With love

Anja

Foreword by Dr. Raymond Keller

Anja Schäfer has written a book on a subject most dear to my heart, that of our sister planet Venus. After the Sun and Moon, Venus is the next brightest object in the early morning or night sky, depending on its position east or west on the horizon along with the rising or setting of the Sun, respectively, as seen from Earth. As such, brilliant Venus has often served as a muse for artists, astronomers, poets, scientists, writers and others from all walks of life. The Co-Founder of the Theosophical Society in 1875, Helena Petrovna Blavatsky (1831-1891), wrote as much about Venus in her famous essay, "History of a Planet," in the September 1887 issue of *Lucifer* (Latin for "Light Bearer") magazine, London, England, Theosophical Society Press:

> *"No star, among the countless myriads that twinkle over the sidereal fields of the night sky, shines so dazzlingly as the planet Venus – not even Sirius-Sothis, the dog-star, beloved by Isis. Venus is the queen among our planets, the crown jewel of our solar system. She is the inspirer of the poet, the guardian and companion of the lonely shepherd, the lovely morning and the evening star. For, stars teach as well as shine."*

The great seeress Blavatsky later went on to explain in her landmark work, *The Secret Doctrine* (London, England: Theosophical Society Press, 1888), that:

"Venus is the most occult, powerful, and mysterious of all the planets; the one whose influence upon, and relation to the Earth is most prominent (Vol 2., p. 30).

"According to the Occult Doctrine, this planet is our Earth's primary, and its spiritual prototype (Vol. 2, p. 31)

"Venus, or Lucifer (also Sukra and Usanas) the planet, is the light-bearer of our Earth, in both its physical and mystic sense (Vol. 2, p. 32).

As the author of seven books, so far, on the glory and mysteries of the planet Venus, I find a wonderful kinship with Anja and her work of love in producing *Venus and I.* She describes her ascent to higher consciousness beginning with meeting Omnec Onec, the Ambassador from Venus, and shortly thereafter coming in contact with the Phaistos Disk, which is permanently on display at the Archaeological Museum in Heraklion, Crete. With Sister Omnec as her mentor and a link to the Cosmos gained through her pondering of the Phaistos Disk, Anja ultimately engaged with a process whereby she discovered her Oversoul and the true path to enlightenment.

For myself, the process was similar. My ascent to higher consciousness began after meeting the Rev. Clayton Parker in 1987, the 87-year-old friend since his boyhood of Annalee Skarin, the author of nine deeply spiritual books who bodily "translated" to Venus from Mt. Shasta, California, in Brother Clayton's presence. Sister Annalee is now known as Lady Encara and resides on a so-called "Super Earth" planet in the Sirius Star Sector known as Belaton, where she presides over a Venusian settlement. Her full story can be found in my first book, *Venus Rising* (Terra Alta, West Virginia: Headline Books, 2015).

Just as for Anja, it wasn't long after I met Clayton that I came in contact with a slew of ancient Egyptian artifacts at a meeting of the Outer Space International Research and Investigations Society (OSIRIS) at a member's home in Murray, Utah, just outside of Salt Lake City. Clayton brought them to the meeting and was demonstrating psychometry, or the process of reading and interpreting ancient artifacts through extrasensory perception. One artifact particularly caught my attention, a facsimile disk drawn on a papyrus that appears in the Book of Abraham, one of the scriptures used in the Church of Jesus Christ of Latter-Day Saints, a.k.a. the "Mormon Church." No sooner had I put my hands on the papyrus, a stream of consciousness came pouring through me to the point where I understood, in contemporary terms, what the disk symbolized. I recognized it immediately as the Kolob Stargate, and provided a detailed analysis of that disk in my *Venus Rising* book.

It is interesting that in both Anja's and my case, the artifact that sparked this awakening was a seer stone. And so it goes, from mentor to artifact, to a deeper understanding of one's place in the Infinite but Living Cosmos. Even as I write this today, 16 May 2023, I received an e-mail concerning Omnec Onec's revelations from a gentleman in Turkey, titled, "Question about souls and bodies they inhabit," which appears below:

> *"Hello Dr. Keller,*
>
> *"I'm an avid follower of your, Omnec Onec's and Rob Potter's contents. I've read all seven books in your Venus Rising series and recently started reading The Gospels of Thomas and Mary Magdalene. Thank you for being a candle in an ocean of darkness and sharing your light with us.*

"I would like to ask this question to Omnec Onec, but since she is unavailable through e-mail, I figured you could also know the answer:

"Omnec Onec has said that the soul moves through mineral, plant, animal and human stages of development and that everything we see around us has a soul. However, some metaphysicians claim that some animals and beings lack a soul. For example, a few refer to Zeta Reticuli Grays as lacking soul.

"Do you or Venusians subscribe to Omnec's view that all material existence carries a soul? Or do you agree with those metaphysicians that say some beings do not have a soul?

"Personally, I think that Omnec's view is more consistent with the divine. Everything having a soul, no matter how primitive or evil, seems a more holistic explanation for creation. However, I simply don't know. Hence my email.

"Thank you for everything and wishing you a pleasant future in light."

Best,

– Berk Ozdalyan, Turkey

Here was my reply, after a careful reading of both Omnec and Anja's books, and insights gained thereby:

Dear Berk,

Many thanks for reading my books. You are much appreciated.

While the focus of Sister Omnec's message is largely on the spiritual aspects of life, my Venus writings are more materialist and Gnostically focused. I agree with Omnec's contention about the evolution of the soul through matter to ever lightening densities. I believe that both matter and spirit are eternal and that life is the inevitable consequence of matter's evolution from the material plane of existence as prompted and imbued by spiritual forces.

With this being the case, the abundant existence of more highly intelligent and sentient life forms throughout the Omniverse is assured.

Your friend always,

– Cosmic Ray

If you count yourself among the millions seeking a greater spiritual enlightenment and understanding, then Anja's *Venus and I* is definitely written specifically for you. Inasmuch as the Moon is the most splendid reflector of the Light of the Sun to the Earth, so also is Anja's *Venus and I* a reflector of the cosmic consciousness one attains from the illumined masters of our sister planet who have come before us.

In the Light of Venus!

– Cosmic Ray

Morgantown, West Virginia, 16 May 2023

Anja's Disclaimer and Acknowledgement for the English edition

I wrote this book originally in my native language German. As mentioned in the preface, it flowed out of me; it practically wrote itself in a period of two weeks. It's written in my typical German style, sometimes with long sentences, occasionally with new word creations and altogether quite with complex information in a very condensed form.

In regards of my planned presence at the Mount Shasta Summer Conference in June 2023, which would take place only a few months later after the sudden flow of writing, and for which I would be preparing myself in my function as a Venus Ambassador, it made sense for me to hopefully be able to present my book in English at this event, if an English translation would be feasible in such a timely manner. Thus, there were only a few weeks to produce an English translation of this relatively complex book.

Thanks to the really good software DeepL as well as thanks to my field of contacts with numerous wonderful people who have been connected with Omnec Onec, me and the Venus information for many years, it was actually possible to create an English translation in a relatively short time and even have it proofread twice.

The version you now hold in your hands is a "readable English edition", in which you may nevertheless occasionally stumble over a German style and German grammar. A translation that is as perfect as if it were written by a native English speaker was impossible to create in such a short time on a volunteer basis.

Please read this book first and foremost with your heart. If possible, please see past and through the language differences in style and expression. If you can do that, this book can be a loving, enriching, joyful inspiration both in content and energy.

At this point, I would like give love, appreciation, and gratitude to the proofreaders who helped me create and publish an English translation of my book at such a rapid pace: Brad Markus, Jonathan Nolan, Rick Keefe, Bill Corkhill, Zandar Schultz, Karoline Weltken, Kun Kelly Zhang, and Dr. Raymond Keller. They all have volunteered a great deal of time to this work. In all humility, I would like to say that they are helping to increase the light on earth both through their own presence and through their participation in this work.

With love and blessings

Anja

May 2023

Acknowledgement for the German edition

I thank my dear parents Renie and Gerhard immeasurably for all they have done for me throughout their lives. They are blessed.

I would like to thank Marianne, Ninja, Kim, Ralph, and Axel for being the first to read my book in its entirety and for helping me with their feedback to correct mistakes and to receive enough encouragement and tailwind to actually take the step into publication.

I would like to thank Reiner Feistle for his trust in me and for giving me the opportunity on August 20, 2022, to give my first public presentation in my function as "Ambassador of the Venusians" at one of his congresses. He and all present know that this was a significant milestone for me. I still don't like labels and – if at all – I use the term "Ambassador of Venus" or "Facilitator of Venusians" with all humility and gratitude and with Omnec Onec's blessing; I only use it to give people an idea of what it's all about.

I especially thank Frank Jacob for his outstanding commitment to translate Robert Potter's presentation into German during our "From Venus with Love Tour 2022" with Dr. Raymond Keller and also for supporting me technically during my presentation at Reiner's Congress. I find Frank's films and his public work as a "Consciousness Archaeologist" very important for seeing through the background powers agenda and for recognizing higher-level connections in world events.

Special thanks also go to Robert Potter. Rob has been a friend or even "fan" of the Venusian Omnec Onec for decades and is very aware of the value of her presence on Earth. His knowledge of Venus is immense. Rob supports the gathering of like-minded Souls and the spread of knowledge of galactic contacts through, among other things, the organization of the Mount Shasta Summer Conferences and his own worldwide activities.

To Werner Forster of the German UFO-Nachrichten magazine, I say thank you for his friendly support in publishing our articles (mine as well as Omnec Onec's and Dr. Raymond Keller's, which I write and translate, respectively). I find his unassuming manner and his many years of consistency in disseminating non-mainstream content to be very valuable to the world.

To my dear Venus teachers and Soul friends Omnec Onec and Dr. Raymond Keller, I thank you infinitely for your wisdom, your love and your patience. From my personal point of view, they are two special angels on this planet.

I dedicate this book to my beloved and to love.

Anja

April 2023

Readers' Comments

This is the initial feedback from my dear first readers, to whom I am so grateful for taking the time to thoroughly read what is, after all, a book quite rich in content.

In the multimedia age this is anything but a matter of course. Intensive reading and immersion in a book is something quite different from watching videos and quickly skimming short impulses in social media channels - not to mention being sprinkled with mainstream media.

These people, whose voices I acknowledged in my book, have given me helpful, honest and loving support. They provided the tailwind which reached me from the right direction and encouraged me to really publish this very personal work.

May this feedback be an appetizer and get you started.

You can read this book, which contains so much knowledge, experience and wisdom, on very different levels: With the mind, with the feeling and with the heart. Each chapter is a small book in itself, with its own theme – guided by a common thread: the personal life story of the author.

Authentic, relentlessly honest with herself and yet full of humor and love, Anja takes you with her on her path of experiences and insights. There is so much knowledge, research and wisdom in the background; excellently implemented in clear, understandable language and never with a raised, instructive finger. This work encourages us to love ourselves and value our own experiences. It also shows creative ways in which we can help shape our future.

I am very grateful for this great wealth of information that will surely inspire and accompany me for a long time.

Kim

Dear Anja,

You take the reader with you on your personal journey through life, you courageously let us participate in your heartfelt journey, you make a great arc from the stages of your insights and your own spiritual awakening process to the great connections of the cosmic plan of creation. Through the ups and downs of your life's path, much wisdom, love and insight has been brought forth in you. You recognize in it the divine providence and make peace with everything. It is pure inspiration for me how you describe your healing path and the continuous opening for the pure true divine love. The intensive work on your life themes and cycles, conclude in love and conscious integration of the knowledge gained in your life.

No matter how tangled, sorrowful, or complicated our Soul journeys may seem, you strengthen the reader in deep trust in the divine guidance that everything serves a perfect plan of creation and thus ultimately the homecoming into divine love.

This book is full of valuable impulses to reconnect with what this planet is really about, the awakening of human beings into their God-given highest consciousness, reconnection with the Divine and Love – our only way back home.

Ninja

In her book, Anja describes an attitude to life that is summed up as follows in Chapter 9: "Being born, running through life, dying. Slowly, it's boring, don't you think? In truth, life is so much bigger. There is so much more to discover, to live, to be."

This attitude towards life is completely in line with today's zeitgeist.

I am sure that many readers will recognize something of their own in Anja's experiences and thought processes. She finds words for what most of us feel today, but in the hectic of everyday life often remain submerged under the surface or not at all comes up.

Ralph

Dear Anja,

Your book is very well done, loving, cheerful and really nice to read. It is my pleasure and honor if my input makes you feel even more confident and comfortable to publish it!

From the bottom of my heart, good luck with it and may the energy you share with this book encourage equally open hearts on their journey and give inspiration to find their own keys, just as you found yours!

Marianne

This book describes the spiritual awakening process of the author. Her refreshing and witty way of writing made me feel like I was on her journey.

A beautiful book that I can only recommend.

Axel

Chapter 1 – The Beginning

Remember, I will still be here
As long as you hold me, in your memory

"Remember Me," song by Josh Groban (2004)

How do you tell a story that has no beginning and no end? No "once upon a time" ...and no ending with the words ... "and they lived happily ever after."

Now my story is not really a fairy tale story either, even though parts of it may seem that way to some. It is also not only MY story, but it is the story of many people on Earth, only that in this case it is told through my personality.

I am writing this book for one simple reason: the day before I left on my trip to Turkey, where I arrived a few hours ago, I took a long walk across the fields in the area where I live. It was cold, around freezing, so I was able to walk well over the almost frozen Earth. As I walked, I suddenly thought about what else I would like to do if I only had a few months to live. Although it is quite unlikely that I will cross over to the spirit world in the summer, this question suddenly occupied my mind.

So I thought about what I still have for open cycles. With which people am I not yet at peace with from my point of view, with whom do I feel that I still have something to clarify? To whom would I still like to share something specific? Are there open wishes that I would still like to fulfill – be it experiences or the acquisition of something? What do I feel I would be missing just before my transition and what would I still need to accomplish?

So the question is: If I were about to leave this Earthly life and this body, would I be free, ready and willing? Could I leave relaxed, grateful and with a blissful smile on my face or would there be unresolved issues that would keep me bound and because of which I would like to return?

With these questions in mind, I walked the Earth in my walking shoes and it clearly crystallized relatively quickly what else I would like to do when I crossed over to the spiritual world in a few months.

Since I had already asked myself this question from time to time earlier in my life and had already fulfilled a great many wishes and completed open cycles, there was indeed not much left that I felt would still bind me. Strictly speaking, and even after repeated, careful consideration, there are only two things at the moment: I would update my will because a change has occurred due to the departure of a longtime friend of mine, and secondly, I would still like to write down my history.

Now I'm not like Achilles, who, if the movie Troy is to be believed, also wanted to go down in world history and be remembered for his downfall. The beautiful title song of the film "Remember Me" describes in the lyrics that one makes oneself immortal by remaining in the memory of people. And since later stories were told about Achilles and his victory over Troy, he did indeed become immortal.

Ambitions of this kind I have not, and yet I feel that my story wants to be told, and even if I write it down only for my beloved, for you, or for God. Or for myself.

So how do I tell a story with no beginning and no end? A cyclical story, a multidimensional story.

I can only jump in and start somewhere and then drift as if in a spiral or a labyrinth.

That's why I'm starting this narrative here in Turkey, because this is where I have been for two weeks now, and one of the reasons I've traveled to this place is to complete a cycle that began 33 years ago.

That's why I find it exciting to listen to myself while I write this book in the course of my stay, because it's not going to be a travelogue, what I'm experiencing here is far too boring on the face of it. My return here after 33 years is only the trigger, the connecting point, where I enter to write my story out of myself.

Already doubts come and I think: Such nonsense, Anja, what are you actually doing? You're not going to finish it, and besides, you'll never get what you want to say across the way you mean it anyway. No one grasps that and they will finish you off, if only by bad reviews on Amazon and not by real stoning or at least egg and tomato throwing.

All right, it doesn't matter. I'm just going to imagine now that I'm telling everything just to myself, my beloved, and God.

My beloved ..., with that we are in the subject concerning my return to Turkey after 33 years. Of course, I do not know what will happen within the next two weeks – but it is not about an external beloved – that is for sure. It is much deeper than that, it is about within, it is about the all-encompassing LOVE.

I have set an intention before this journey. The intention for this journey is that I will arrive at my turning point and from that point on my journey will be inward.

For thousands of years, I have been breathing myself out. For thousands of years, since my first incarnation on Earth, since I chose to journey through oblivion and reincarnations, I have been exhaling. I spend myself. Through oblivion, through separation from God. I was born in diverse bodies, didn't know anymore who I was, made my experiences, suffered from all kinds of things that being human in the darkened consciousness brings with it and that I have in common with probably several billion people on Earth and died sooner or later – in the earlier centuries rather sooner than later. We rarely reached old age. Mostly we died of malnutrition, torture, war, suicide, murder, broken heart or illness and went back to the spiritual world, usually without having remembered who we really are.

We accumulated karma through our unconsciousness. Karma is the law of cause and effect and has nothing to do with guilt, certainly not with guilt and atonement and God-punishment or similar non-sense. Karma as a cosmic law that says what I send out returns to me. Moreover, as a Soul, I have the inner desire to have all experiences from all perspectives so that one day I will become completely round and perfect. I cannot be perfect on the outer levels as long as I still lack experience or at least the acceptance of all experiences and of everything that is. As long as I judge and feel detached, I am not round. From this point of view, this journey could also be called an inward spiralization, because deep inside I am perfect, I am round, I am one with all that is. But since I have chosen to exhale, to travel through the levels of consciousness into the lower worlds, I also experience myself in polarity, in forgetting, in separation and in apparent imperfection.

I feel I am approaching the roundness. That is why I am here, that is why I have set this intention. If you read these lines and think: Such nonsense, Anja is as far away from being round as the sun is from the Andromeda galaxy or even further – well, these are YOUR thoughts. And if you want to keep yourself separated from me in this way, by thinking to be able to judge about where I am in my consciousness and on my journey as Soul, then it is probably better, you put the book aside again or throw it away.

If, on the other hand, you are also on your life journey and would like to increase your self-knowledge by possibly finding yourself in one or the other of what I am telling here as well as in the vibrations between the lines, then stay with me and come along. Accompany me, I have so many beautiful things to tell. It will be exciting, interesting, maybe sometimes a bit seemingly tragic or sad, and hopefully it will be humorous and inspiring. Possibly also instructive, because you may not know one or the other yet.

So what happened 33 years ago here in Turkey, in Side to be exact, that I think I came back here to complete a cycle? I was 20 years old and had just graduated from high school. My mother invited me to go on a trip with her as a reward, so we flew here for a week. It was the only trip in my life that I took with my mother alone. It was very hot, even the sea was warmer than I have experienced any sea since. But it was also in August. I don't remember much, only the most important thing, and that was Mustafa, who worked at the reception. I remember that he really wanted to meet me. My mother found him sympathetic and didn't stand in the way, so after a few days he and I went out together. Somehow we got together and fell in love. The week was over quickly and I remember I was crestfallen to have to go back to Germany, and he was sad too. So we kept in close contact and talked on the phone a lot when I got back to Berlin. We really liked each other, so after a short time, I think after two weeks, I went back to Side and moved in with him in his mini-room in a shared apartment behind the hotel. I didn't have much money, it was just enough for this flight and some stay. Mustafa and I were quite happy together, we got along well and had a good time together. In his sparse free time, we went on excursions. We visited the lime terraces of Pamukkale and a concert of the Turkish singer Sezen Aksu in an amphitheater. After about four weeks, my parents cut me off. They did not want to support my budding lottery life with a Turk and indirectly forced me to come back to Germany. Since Mustafa didn't have much money and only this job in the hotel, we had no idea how to manage our relationship. I was obviously not in love, not creative and not brave enough to defy my parents and so Mustafa and I said goodbye to each other after five weeks. I can still see him looking somber at the airport, he really liked me, he was really sad that I was leaving. I was sad too and I didn't want it to be over. When I got back to Berlin, we kept in touch and I invited him to come to Germany. But it wasn't meant to be and we lost touch after about a year.

These eyes, mine anyway, almost fell out of my head when Mustafa sent me a friendship request via Facebook after 22 years, which must have been in spring 2012.

At that time, I was already living at Lake Constance and had already moved from Berlin to Landshut, from Landshut to Mönchengladbach, and from Mönchengladbach to Lake Constance, when suddenly this message arrived by email. At that time, I still got Facebook notifications by email, which was in the very early days.

In any case, I was completely blown away and really believed that the circles of destiny now wanted to put us together after 22 years, so that we could pick up where we left off back in Turkey, and that we would finally become a happy couple.

For good reasons, which however I only became aware of much later, I had remained single. Only between 1997 and 1999 there was one more man with whom I had some kind of relationship, but that was a karmic story and from my point of view had little to do with love. In other words, after the short episode with Mustafa in Turkey, there was no other man with whom it felt good on both sides. This does not mean that it was my conscious decision to live partnerless – not at all, rather the opposite – I was always looking for the right man for me and only today do I grasp why this urge to find my man was so immense from my innermost being. The depth of this will be revealed in the course of this book. LOVE in all its facets was and is one of my great life themes and the realm of experience, thanks to which I was allowed to suffer the most deeply and thanks to which I grew and matured the most intensively.

Against this background of unredeemed singlehood, I was extremely sensitive and had a single heap of hope. Hope for LOVE. The idea that Mustafa would just love to see me again – just like that, with no expectations, no promises, no marriage – that didn't even cross my mind. For me, his appearance after so many years was the beginning of coming home to the ultimate relationship. The miracle of fate and the closing of an open cycle seemed perfect for me, especially since Mustafa also happened to live in Zurich, only 100 kilometers away from me!

That he was married to a Swiss woman and had a teenage son, he did not tell me in the chat and I did not ask about it. I had to decorate my inner illusion building optimally, in order to be able to run correctly into the knife. Only by denying all realities I could really feel my glass castle of built illusions breaking inside me. Quite apart from that: Of course it happens that people get divorced and enter into a partnership with another love – that happens all the time. But our Souls were not meant for each other as a couple in this life, our re-encounter was only meant for a certain, very important experience, but not to become a couple. If the couple theme had been in the field at all, then I would have met the whole re-encounter quite differently in terms of energy and frequency, namely much more relaxed, more serene, just easy going and not with such a giant glass castle inside me.

The physical encounter between us came after two weeks of Facebook contact on my initiative. In retrospect, I find it important that I was the one who requested the meeting, not him. My Soul obviously wanted to get it over with as quickly as possible – the painful lesson of disappointment. So we met in Schaffhausen, which is pretty much near each of us, in a parking lot.

When we arrived at the meeting point at the same time and saw each other again after such a long time, it was a great joy on both sides. Both of us were very changed in appearance, I quite overweight, he with a small belly and by now gray-haired, only his gap in his teeth was still the same, we fell into each other's arms and held each other for minutes. His knees were vibrating. The energetic exchange was mega intense.

That's exactly WHAT this reunion was about – this energy exchange. What it ultimately did to Mustafa, I don't know, but for me it was a milestone on my journey back home to LOVE. How I mean that, you will not fully understand at this point, that will bubble up in the further course of this book.

After our long embrace and intense exchange of feelings, we started talking to each other. That's when I learned that after we broke up, Mustafa met a Swiss woman in Turkey, moved in with her in Switzerland, married her and has a son with her. Just to know THAT broke everything in me. I felt the glass lock inside me crack and break and I could no longer stand there and talk with Mustafa, I was so disappointed. Sure, I had a huge expectation and so it came to a huge disappointment. Apart from that, nobody knows whether he and I would have been a good match at all, we could never find out. But since everything in God's plan is right as it is, we would certainly not have fit together – we were simply not meant to come together as life companions in this life, otherwise it would have worked out! And nevertheless the meetings were super important for me, because Mustafa is, in my life the only man, whom I can classify in the category

"Soul partner[1]", even if we lived no partnership together. But from the feeling he was and is among all the numerous men that I have met in the course of my life, the only man with whom I felt a mutual feeling of closeness and sympathy at eye level. I can well imagine that in former lives we were together as Soul mates and that therefore we shared such a basic love, a basic attraction. Of the giant divine LOVE, which I was also allowed to experience and I will come back to it later in detail, nevertheless there can be no question here. And all other man-woman-stories in my life were, if I want to pigeonhole them, most likely karmic connections in different variations and served to dissolve energetic bonds and to break encrusted belief- and thought-structures.

Now, here in the hotel, the power has just gone out and come back on five times in the last half hour. Click – clack – click – clack. I'm about to go to the reception desk and ask if this is usual here ... I'm about to go nuts! This is worse than in India, there I have also experienced in 2019 the constant power outages – but not every minute!

After meeting Mustafa again after 22 years, I was sick for four weeks – I was really depressed. I still remember that I had two girlfriends visiting me, who had to hold my hand – the first two weeks my friend Claudi was with me, who had to hold the hand of Verena, who then sat by my side for another two weeks. Slowly things started to get better for me, thanks to the support and compassion of these friends. It was really painful to experience heartache because of shattered illusions, and yet after the deep valley of the Soul there was an upwind that let me run into new experiences.

1 With "Soul partner" I mean quite personally the only embodied Soul, which has appeared again and again in the time frame of several decades and with which I feel an inwardly constant, friendly connection – in contrast to "karmic partners", with which the encounters and inner connections feel rather short and completed (from hours to some years). The "twin flame" or also the "(inner) beloved" is something completely different and I talk about it in more detail in the chapters "Initiations" and "Twin Flames".

In hindsight, it strikes me that after this experience, due to a disappointed illusion, I have never again suffered so deeply – differently by all means, but no longer with the depth of a real depression.

The suffering that was triggered by the re-encounter with Mustafa broke open structures in me so that more light could enter. After that I could open up to the next level of experience with the masculine. Far away from LOVE in partner matters and far away from experiencing something HAPPY in this respect. Today I know why this was so and that everything is just right as it is out of pure LOVE. The reasons for this have to do with my Soul plan, which is about returning home to love, to true, divine love. Perhaps you too carry this longing, this subtle memory of divine love within you – I can assure you, it exists, it is absolutely real. In the further course of this book I will circle around love again and again and also dedicate a separate chapter to it.

Today I have returned to Turkey to close once and for all the open cycle that is perhaps the most important for me, by which I mean the open cycle of the search for love in a partnership with a man. This is about the withdrawal of all projections and the end of the program of looking for love in the wrong places, or as Abraham Hicks put it in English: "Looking for Love in all the wrong places."

The realization that I would not find love in a partnership, I had already in 2019, but at that time this realization had not yet flowed through all my lower bodies. So I cannot exactly explain at the moment, but I think a realization begins in the spiritual, in the Soul and that does not mean directly and exclusively that all lower bodies equally already feel and think the same. There may still be old patterns, traumas or other issues that need to be felt again in the course of time, packed in love and let go.

My realization that I am done with the search for a partner came relatively late, after all, I was already 49 years old in 2019. But for that, it was absolutely and irrevocably real. By then, in my own way and at my own pace, I had gone through everything that it IS NOT, that is, what did NOT lead me to the partnership I apparently wanted. I knew it would take a radical change and that change for me was first of all arriving at the point of liberation from this search. This was not a liberation out of defiance or being offended with God or something, no, it was an honest conclusion of a level of experience, because I was able to say with my head held high, clearly before myself and God, "Should there still be a man for me in this life, who is meant for me and who fits me right and I fit him, then I am ready to meet him – and if not, then I remain partnerless and live my life fulfilled, as it is intended in accordance with the divine will and me as a Soul. From this point on, I no longer settle for crumbs, no longer run after a man, and no longer search. From now on, there will be no more compromises, no more affairs either – "only true love." In reality, I had never wished for anything else, the only problem was that I was not yet ready to receive this high love and first had to experience and resolve all kinds of karmic stuff in order to recognize myself and be able to open up and surrender to true love. My Soul simply prevented half things. False, disharmonious partnerships or the founding of a family would have led me into new ties and obligations instead of releasing ties and false programs. Strictly speaking, wrong partnerships and family patterns would have cost me time and energy, which I should spend for this life with other contents – namely for experiencing and recognizing myself and for finding and fulfilling my life task, which has to do with Venus and the transmission of her messages of love and spiritual teachings.

During my Mustafa depression in 2012, I disconnected the Facebook friendship with him again, it was too painful to keep in touch with him. It was just hopeless for me at the time because of the separation illusion, but I wasn't fully aware of that, I wasn't above it. I had to suffer through it and integrate it, and at that time I could only do that by separating on the outside and breaking off contact again. I remember that I had the feeling that this was also painful or upsetting for Mustafa in another way, as I reacted. I felt sorry for him too, but I just had to take care of myself and my reaction and withdrawal was just authentic. A partnership was out of the question and it wasn't meant to be, so I had to suck the pearls out of this sour oyster and the only way to do that was to separate again and by opening myself up to the next level of experiences with men, which actually followed after a few months of processing, after being persuaded by my friend Claudi to sign up on a dating site and slowly start accepting lighter contacts and having looser experiences. Not painless, not without hopes, not without dramas, but little by little it became easier. At some point I realized that I created these experiences for myself to release energetic ties that I had brought into this life – it's about freedom and finding true love – and true love is FREE.

This tells the essence around Mustafa and my time in Side, which is now going into the final phase 33 years after my return to this place, and which was the reason why I started writing this book in the first place.

No more power outages for the last ten minutes – maybe the house's power grid has now gotten used to my energy and remains stable ... let's hope so.

Maybe at this point you don't yet understand what I mean by cyclical existence and what my Turkey story and this book have to do with it and with coming home to LOVE, what it all boils down to and what you might have to do with it. It doesn't matter. There is no beginning and no end and

I'm not getting at anything in particular. Perhaps one reason for telling my story is that in this way I am emptying my inner vessel and offering you a chalice filled with my Soul nectar.

Chapter 2 – The Ring of Destiny

Words are symbols.

Nothing that is true needs to be explained.

This is exciting now. I feel the first chapter is finished and I write the words "Chapter 2." Promptly, the expression "The ring of destiny is closing" comes to my mind. There is a story that wants to be unpacked that I did not think of before I wrote the words "Chapter 2".

So now I know what I want to tell next, namely the story about the ring of destiny closing.

It was in the city of Mönchengladbach in 2001, when I was working at the Birgert company as an assistant to the sales manager. At that time one day suddenly the text "The ring of destiny is closing ... the ri-ing of des-ti-ny- is closing ..." sang in me in a mantra form. Repeating themselves over and over. These words simply fell into my head, and that was triggered by the fact that my grandfather on my mother's side had lived in Mönchengladbach, that I had often been to that city as a child, and that fate had brought me back to that city a few decades later without any connection to my Earthly family.

And yet it was my life path, a part of my journey, for whatever reason, there was some energy from the side of my family, and then I landed exactly there to have experiences, to close the fate ring, to complete a cycle and in 2004 to probably leave this city finally behind me.

The story around Mönchengladbach, the company Birgert and the magic sales manager is a story that started somewhere in Atlantis. Yes, why should I not hit the nail on the head, because for me that is actually so, from my own memories.

What I experienced in Mönchengladbach in the field of this company and at the side of this man reminded me of the darkest time of the deepest Soul I have ever experienced. It reminds me of the time when the black magicians in Atlantis extracted their Souls from the enlightened people. Leaving this company after 13 months of employment, I was internally in an experience of ultimate panic, in a state of consciousness where I was in absolute fear for my Soul. I felt as far away from the light as it is possible to be just before destruction. My innermost being was in a constant search mode for a safe place in the universe and found none. I felt naked in the infinity of space or like a polar bear that had lost its fur. I had the feeling that if I was not saved inwardly now, my Soul would be lost. I felt completely sucked out. Maybe it was an illusion, but then it was perfect. Or maybe it was really a true memory of a time when something like that happened – and where I was a part of it – in what disguise or role, I don't know.

All I know is that I could only pray. That was the only thing that remained for me and that probably saved me and ultimately led me out of the inner situation. I had never prayed before, certainly not the Lord's Prayer, but at that time I was glad that I remembered this prayer. I thought it over and over again. Externally, I had just experienced a nervous breakdown, had turned my back on the company for good, and had arrived at my apartment after the initial emergency treatment in a clinic. There, the symptoms of the nervous breakdown returned and I waited for my friend Claudi and for the emergency doctor. I had lockjaw and my whole body was under high tension. Lockjaw means that my neck had turned to one side and was stuck there and I couldn't get my jaws apart. I had no control over myself, at least it was only hanging by a thread, that's why the blessing was the ultimate, that I remembered the Lord's Prayer and that my friend Claudi came and then at some point also the totally annoyed emergency doctor, who luckily gave me the right injection at the end, which led to the relaxation of my muscles and the calming of my nerves.

I remember that Claudi sat at my bedside and held my hand until I slowly calmed down a bit and at some point I fell asleep after the low point had been overcome both internally and externally. I think it was also on that day when I called my parents, who were already living on Lake Constance, in the afternoon and my mother checked it on the phone that I was at the end, without me saying it. She said to my father, "She's having a nervous breakdown," and then the two of them promptly jumped into their car and drove the 600 kilometers up to me in Mönchengladbach, packed me up the next day, and I was once again the little kid who, at 32, was hanging in the trunk of Dad's big Chrysler Voyager with a packed bag like a sip of water and I was glad to be safe now.

I tell this absolutely and not at all to press a tear-jerker here or to make myself important with some Soul drama, the story is much bigger and cyclical, like everything I try to describe here.

Because my experiences with the boss in this company, whose nicknames in the company were, by the way and quite honestly, "Lord of Darkness" and "the Magician", corresponded to the other side of the coin known as the "Phaistos Disc".

I'll go into more detail about the Phaistos Disc in a later chapter, but here are a few facts in case you don't know it:

The Phaistos Disc is a clay discus stamped on both sides, found in 1908 during excavations in the Minoan palace of Phaistos in southern Crete and exhibited in the Archaeological Museum of Heraklion.

It has a diameter of 15 cm and a thickness of 3 cm. Among the so-called experts it is considered indecipherable because it is unique. There is no other find in the world that bears the same symbols and there are no comparisons with other languages, such as the Rosetta Stone, which bears the same text in ancient Greek, demotic and hieroglyphics, and that is why it was possible to decipher hieroglyphics.

Image 1: Phaistos Disc

Discovered in 1908 in Phaistos, Southern Crete. Permanently exhibited in the Archaeological Museum, Heraklion, Crete, Greece.

I am not an archaeological expert, I am a different kind of expert in the matter of the Phaistos Disc, because I know and understand it – in my own way.

And in my own way I knew from the moment I first saw it – and IT ME – that it is not readable or decipherable in an Earthly language because it is multidimensional. I still agree with most of the statements of Dr. Raymond Keller and Dirk Seufert who recognized it as a multidimensional library (Dirk) or as a seer stone (Ray).

The Phaistos Disc is – that's how I see it – a relic from Atlantis with memory codes. It is a universal information carrier and it is multidimensional. Everybody reads his own history in it, everybody experiences it differently and everybody is right. But, of course, it does not speak to everyone at all times. Some saw the discus in the museum a long time ago and didn't react to it, become aware of it again until some decades later either through me or in some other way and boom – something happens in them all of a sudden. Others don't react to it at all, probably because they have nothing to do with the story of Atlantis or because they experience other memory codes in this life or none at all because they didn't sign up for remembering and awakening with Mother-Father-God in the first place.

In any case, the discus has two sides and both sides are different. Most of the symbols are the same, but the arrangement is different. For example, in the center of one side, which I call the day side or light side, and which I experienced first, and BEFORE my dark experience with the Prince of Darkness, there is an eight-petaled flower with a seed. In the center of the other side, which I call the anti-day side or the dark side, there is a rounded triangle with a wave in the center.

I have never tried to interpret the individual symbols or translate the whole discus into language. I know that sounds totally crazy, but for me it is that I AM the discus. The energy of the discus has merged so deeply with me as a Soul and I have experienced both one side and the other personally and deep within me in real terms over a period of several years. Since then, the discus has been practically within me and I radiate its energy myself – but of course only to those who resonate with it – just as the discus in the museum does not have an effect or radiance on every visitor.

After I experienced the dark side in the Birgert company – and this was not only related to the boss, but to the whole company structure, all employees – I also experienced something there, which is called mobbing today – I knew that I could only experience and survive this deep darkness, because I had experienced the light side before. I had to shoot up high and be completely identified with the light, my Soul essence and the divine love, so to speak, in order to be able to dive down into the depth and to rise up again from it and to settle in the middle in the course of my further life. I do not want to anticipate too much, but I will tell all this in the further course of this book and also that the integration of the experiences of the Phaistos Disc ultimately took 22 years – 22 years measured in linear time – and I know this because I experienced my next initiation in the year 2022. In the years immediately following the discus experience, I felt that experiencing this consciousness was enough for this lifetime and that I could not use and integrate more. I agreed to spend the rest of my life integrating and balancing what I had experienced – and, and this is the essence, hopefully someday re-awakening and consciously raising my energy to experience and stabilize Phaistos consciousness again. Phaistos consciousness is oneness consciousness, absolute oneness with the Creator and with all that is, absolute bliss, total creativeness and God-connectedness. The Christ energy is also contained here, I will come back to this later when I tell you more about my light experience with the discus.

Apparently my spiritual guidance saw to it that after 22 years I was integrated enough to be able to receive and unpack the next codes and experience the next cycle of unity consciousness one level deeper. That's where I'm at right now, that's also why I'm in Turkey. I am not only here to complete the Mustafa-Partner-Love-Theme cycle, although I myself do not even know exactly what that means, because I am still in the middle of experiencing it. I have the feeling that I am living several lives in one to the end and am completing open cycles to arrive again in my consciousness as an awakened Soul, stably anchored in the remembered, awake BEING IN LOVE, as an awakened Divine-Feminine – and that with a stable nervous system, with calmness and equanimity, in self-love and mindfulness. That sounds like a huge claim, and it is. In my experience, it takes a lot of work to awaken and remain stable in an enlightened state of consciousness.

In other words, it's about arriving in the zero-point zone, in the present moment.

I don't believe that once awakened always means awakened, it means still having a daily routine, always aligning with God within, always meeting new challenges, always doing inner work, even if it's just remembering or jumping off the thought train to always arrive in the NOW. The train of thought is running non-stop anyway and constantly takes you along again. I believe that the path of spiritual mastery is not an easy one and if you see and experience it differently, congratulations. But I'm sure we can agree on one thing: everyone is an individual, and even if there are divine laws and similarities or specific symptoms on the path of awakening, it is still individual.

I am not telling my story to convince anyone of anything. Maybe I tell it because I finally CAN do it now. I can write and type, I can proofread and correct myself, I can typeset and publish my own book. So if I CAN do it, why shouldn't I DO it? If I were an artist or a musician, then I would want to express just as much what wants to come out of me and with every emptying of my vessel God could pour something in, which I let stew in my alchemical cauldron and can bring again into the outside world.

I'm sure I'll contradict myself, add to myself, or correct myself at times. This is not a perfect text written here by a perfect woman. It is the imperfect in the perfect that is expressed. Words can never perfectly reflect something, they can only transport energies. What is true cannot be described in words. What is true needs no explanation.

That is why the Phaistos Disc is true. It is not decipherable. Luck! Really – it's good luck that it is indecipherable, and I am sure that it is with intention.

If it was decipherable, there would be clever scientists who would claim that so and so is the meaning of its language. No, the discus laughs about it! It says: You can grimace your teeth out at me! Either you grasp me intuitively, with your heart and with your Soul, or I am for you only an interesting thing from clay which is exhibited in a glass box in a museum.

Chapter 3 – The Imperfect in the Perfect

People who think they are enlightened
have lost their minds.

Well, never mind,
leave the mind behind and
then you are enlightened.

– Omnec Onec

The imperfect in the perfect – that's how I experienced myself at my peak in the experience of the Phaistos Disc day side in 2000. I preferred to dress in a way to express my inner self through my clothing. I went shopping and bought only clothes that expressed two aspects of my being: Something disharmonious within the harmonious and something androgynous.

This phase lasted for a few months and as my material grounding including financial grounding became thinner and thinner, my shopping experiences were limited to a few specific pieces.

For example, I had a shirt in which one shoulder was cut differently than the other. I had a red dress that I had black straps sewn on so it was two-tone. Then I had androgynous pants, which were white shorts that had a kind of flap in the front so that the pants looked like a miniskirt from the front and like pants from the back. I also paid scrupulous attention to my underwear, it always had to be perfectly imperfect as well. I don't have all these items anymore, but I remember that I always dressed in the morning according to my feeling in a certain color or color combination and then had experiences that day that were in harmony with it. For example, I once had a white and blue day, wearing a blue dress with white shoes and walking around with a white bag. When I was in this outfit in an ice cream parlor to nibble an ice cream, then suddenly only people came in there who were also dressed in white-blue. I had it the same way with a black and red day and with other color days as well.

In this extreme time, I would speak onto cassettes. I knew that I was going through a phase of enlightenment and that I was experiencing something special, so I wanted to record it and recorded the cassettes. Besides, at that time I was feeling blissful and in the all-oneness, but outwardly seemed more and more alone, because in my environment at that time it was definitely a pure overload. That's why I amused myself by speaking on my cassettes and listening to them again afterwards.

Since I am not in this extreme energy now at this moment, I cannot reflect all experiences let alone transmit this energy optimally through my words, I can always only tell excerpts, when they arise into my conscious mind. They will make sense again when considered as a whole, because they belong altogether in the narration of the cyclic existence.

What I experienced in the year 2000 triggered by the disc, by the day side of the disc, mind you, was a remembrance of a magical state of consciousness from the high times of Atlantis. I felt the creation of experiences in a playful way, but I had no control over it and therefore could not ground it, integrate it or balance it within me. For this I needed the years and decades afterwards. I downloaded, so to speak, a huge portion of memory codes into my system, which were gradually unpacked over time and found their place in me.

In retrospect, it occurs to me that I was not able to deal with all of this – after my fall from the state of enlightenment, if you will – working consciously with it. There was not yet enough peace and presence in me to be able to do something like INNER WORK with myself. Also, there was no therapist, coach or colleague of experience I could have confided in and who could have helped me through it in order to integrate what I had experienced in a more relaxed and perhaps also faster way. In my personal case, this was obviously not supposed to be – I had to go through it alone and because I am guided by LOVE and always had at least one wonderful friend in my life, it worked out. In this respect it is not true that I had to go through it all alone, I mean "without professional help".

LOVE, that is the divine presence or my Oversoul, an absolutely wonderful, love-filled intelligence, controls all experiences. It guides me through my whole life and you through your whole life. It is perfect. Everything we experience is perfectly orchestrated by a higher intelligence.

I have come to the realization that everything that is, is absolutely perfect. What seems imperfect is just my view, my perspective, because I usually or mostly don't see the whole picture. This is why it is so ultimately important to surrender to divine guidance and to go over and over again into stillness and into the zero-point zone, because only there does everything fall into place and the point of cyclical and linear existence converge in one. Only in this point I can sense or grasp the overview. This is not to be grasped with the mind at all. Also these words are imperfect. But if they remind me and you that we are really and truly substantially more than our thinking, feeling, sensual grasping and more than our body, then they have fulfilled their purpose, if there is one.

The Phaistos Disc is also something imperfect in the perfect. It is by all means crooked and awry, it is visibly made by hand. But the creator was not concerned with perfection in craftsmanship. The creator was concerned with imprinting his energy into the clay, his multi-dimensional energy. For the creator of the Disc knew that Atlantis and the enlightened consciousness would fall and that she would forget herself on her future journey through the ages and through the incarnations. He knew that, like Hansel and Gretel in the forest, he would need something to remember who he really was one day in the future. She knew that one day in the future the Disc and the essence of her own existence would come together again, because in truth they are ONE, and that then she would remember everything again little by little. He knew that when he found himself within the Disc again, he was on the fast train home.

Chapter 4 – The Dark Crystal

Hold her, for she is a part of you.

¬ Enlightened Master to Jen in the movie "The Dark Crystal"

The Dark Crystal is a 1982 movie created by Frank Oz and the Muppets production team. It is one of my favorite movies because it is so beautifully done with the characters having real people in them. Most of all, I love the story because it reminds me of my own. I'm sure the screenwriter of THE DARK CRYSTAL had intuitions, because the story this movie tells is at least symbolically true from my point of view. It is the story of Atlantis, of the breaking apart of the high beings who had fallen out of unity consciousness and from that moment on broke in two – just like the dark crystal. They caused a splinter to be broken out of the crystal and from that moment on there were two different characters in the world, two entities, separated from each other but yet in truth one. There were the cold, cruel Skeksis, whose favorite pastimes were lavish feasting, domination, destruction, and sucking the lifeblood out of other beings, preferably the Gelflings. And then there were the gentle Urus, dedicated to the ancient mystical methods of wisdom with their chants and teachings. The Skeksis represented the distorted, disturbed masculine aspect of being, and the Urus the feminine aspect of being, which maintained wisdom within themselves and lived quietly, peacefully, and gently by themselves as the guardians of knowledge. The two beings never met each other, they were the essences of the disintegrated being of unity. But the Earth was ruled by the nasty Skeksis, who had nothing else in mind than to keep dominating the world even after the approaching great conjunction of the three great suns. The only thing the Skeksis were afraid of was that the prophecy could come true and the crystal could be healed again by the hand of a Gelfling. For this reason, the Skeksis had all the Gelflings killed, they wanted to prevent at all costs losing their position of power.

But of course, as it must be in a story, where in the end the light and love are the victors, because in truth there is no other way, so of course one Gelfling had survived, or more precisely, two Gelflings, a boy and a girl, whose fate it was to find each other and together walk the path of the crystal shard and heal the great crystal in the dark castle of the Skeksis.

I am always so touched when, in the final scene, the Gelfling girl Kira is killed by a blow from a Skeksis fighting for her life, and brave Jen still takes the final step and puts the crystal shard into the great crystal – even though he seems to have just lost the only being he loves, his second half. But Jen knows that the crystal must be healed so that the world is once again free from the evil rule of the tyrannical Skeksis. What else would happen in the final moments, even Jen didn't know – and it's just so beautiful!

The great crystal is healed and the three suns combine into one ray – the great conjunction goes into resonance with the crystal, which is now a light crystal again. At the same time the Urus, who had set up in a circle around their Twin Souls, the Skeksis, merge with their counterparts. They merge with each other and become once again the luminous, great, sublime, beautiful beings of light that they once were.

They are one again. And as a blessing and out of gratitude, the great Souls bring Kira back to life and say at the end: Hold her close, for she is a part of you. In the light of the crystal now create your world.

And then the healed light beings all ascend together.

Sigh – I even have tears in my eyes when I write down these memories of the film. I feel so deeply connected to it, because from my point of view it contains everything that we humans on Earth are going through right now. And it reminds me of my shattered being, because I too remembered back in 2000 my being as a great, light-filled, androgynous being that was completely one. I can remember energetically feeling about ten feet tall and complete within myself. I had arrived deeply within me, it was a great love experience of my own oneness.

But it didn't last, I fell out of that state of consciousness again. The essential thing was that I remembered and from that moment on I knew that this was the truth and that I would not strive for anything else in this life or in any future life but to return to this perfect state of being and to consecrate to it.

It was like a kind of foretaste and at the same time it was a recollection.

This ascent of consciousness had begun with the Phaistos Disc. And before the Phaistos Disc I had met my teacher from Venus, Omnec Onec, so the ascent had rather begun through the meeting with her. Yes, where is the beginning?

In any case, these two triggers caused my first awakening experiences in this life. They are connected with each other, but even today I do not have the complete overview. I only know that in the year 2022, that is 22 years after the first remembering of my perfect being as an androgynous light being, I experienced a remembering of my remembering and that I had thus arrived at the same cyclic point of the journey through my existence.

Chapter 5 – Atlantis

At the time of Atlantis, this sacred map home, to abiding perpetual remembrance of our divinity was tampered with and this created significant confusion for God's children. Indeed, this is what we are all awakening from and recorrecting right now in this time of Mother Earth's Great Ascension.

It is so important that memories of Atlantis are brought out of the unconscious because it reminds us that we are truly multi-dimensional avatar beings and we are blessed with the innate ability to time travel back to the time of any period, including Atlantis and Lemuria. We are able do this in order to rescript and restore those timelines, whereby extremely deep, traumatic incidents took place.

¬ Jen McCarty, "Twin Flames and the Event"

There is a lot of literature about Atlantis. For science Atlantis still belongs to the realm of legends and if someone is looking for it at all, then they are looking for the physical evidence of Atlantis.

The physical doesn't matter. What is essential is the energy, the experiences that the Souls on Earth had at that time and that have been imprinted in the ether of the chronicles.

It is no coincidence that many incarnate Souls are drawn to and engaged with the Atlantis theme.

I found the most profound correspondences of my own experiences and intuitive knowledge while reading the book "Twin Flames and the Event" by Jen McCarty. The quotes inserted at the beginning of this chapter give an impression of the depth of the information that Jen has been transmitted by her spiritual team and thanks to which she describes connections in simple words, with which I am very much in resonance internally and where I constantly felt while reading: Yes, that's exactly how I know it, that's what I remember as a Soul.

I have never dealt with Atlantis out of intellectual interest, because I know that the narratives from human sources mostly differ from each other. That I became aware of Jen McCarty's book shows me again that the information that is important somehow finds its way to you at the right time – just as perhaps you are holding this book in your hands at just the right time for you. Also, I have never been interested in other Venus sources after I had Omnec Onec personally in my life and her spiritual teachings fulfilled me. It wasn't until 2021, when I met Venus historian Dr. Raymond Keller, that there was an expansion of knowledge for me followed by the next initiation. I will come back to Ray in a later chapter when I tell more about the Venus Ambassadors.

After my first two initiations through Omnec Onec and the Phaistos Disc, I was busy integrating the knowledge I had received, while at the same time trying to keep my Earth life as stable as possible – there was no room in me for further Venus or Atlantis information or other spiritual knowledge from other sources.

Therefore, I don't know anything about Atlantis from written knowledge. I only know what I have experienced, and when I suddenly felt an Atlantis resonance through the Phaistos Disc, that is, when I knew inwardly that the Disc had something to do with Atlantis, I was surprised myself. It was intuitive knowledge.

The descriptions of Jen McCarty in her book "Twin Flames and the Event" fill memory gaps in me and I am very glad that thanks to her clear descriptions and meditations I found keys for healing the wounds of separation.

I am speaking here about Atlantis, what I think I know and what I remember psychically:

A long time ago I came to Earth with my Soul brothers and sisters. We were fully conscious light beings of the higher dimensions. We were not yet physical. Why did we actually come? Perhaps in response to some kind of invitation or out of curiosity. Perhaps also to populate the Earth with life forms. It was not our intention in the first place to incarnate physically or to stay long. But the energy of the Earth became so physical in frequency, so third-dimensional, that our frequency gradually adjusted. By slowing down the frequency, we entered duality. We attracted lower-frequency realms of experience, and thus the positive and the negative emerged. From negativity came division and from division came discord, disunity and strife. From this followed the ultimate separation from the high God consciousness and we became physical. In between there is still the polarization of the forces into male and female. In the physical we embodied ourselves in male and in female bodies. We entered into relationships with others and by falling in vibration and entering lower consciousness we began to create karma. We were subject to the law of cause and effect and then we got stuck in the reincarnation cycles.

Somehow and at some point, genetic manipulation also comes in here or it ran parallel. By this I mean the interference of another race in the events of the Earth in order to subjugate humans and to erase their memory of their true, high Soul nature. It cannot be erased from the Soul, but when the Soul incarnates in physical bodies whose brains have separate cerebral hemispheres and whose DNA has been stripped down to the minimum, the embodied Soul no longer knows who it is and where it comes from. Instead, it identifies itself with the physical and with the consciousness of separation. It is only a matter of survival for it, of satisfying the basic needs and thus it is the perfect victim for forces that like to suck out the life essence in order to assimilate it and maintain their own sham existence. Just as the Skeksis in THE DARK CRYSTAL suck and imbibe the life essence of other beings in order to refresh their own existence, strengthen themselves and extend their lifespan in the physical.

A nasty game so to speak – and nevertheless it is true. And nevertheless it is *not unfortunately* true, because everything is just as permitted in the great, divine plan for the experiences and developments of the Souls.

Actually, this is also all I know about Atlantis at the moment.

For me, the essential thing is that through my encounter with the Phaistos Disc, these memories came to life in me and I realized that I would now start the journey home.

However, who are the Gelflings? Who heals the broken crystal?

Chapter 6 – The Phaistos Disc

Symbols are words.

Nothing that is true needs to be explained.

Now it becomes difficult. But it is time for me to tell the story of the Phaistos Disc as I have experienced it. If and when it will be fully revealed to me one day, exactly when and how and why it was made, I do not know. I am sure that by looking at a timeline, by reading in the chronicle, it is possible to bring all this vividly into the counter present in pictures. I do not have this ability yet, nor do I need to know more.

I have complete trust in the fact that always exactly the knowledge reveals itself to me as knowledge, which I really need and which I can also process. In the end, it must fit into the head, so that the brain and language can process and pass on the knowledge. Otherwise it makes no sense, if it is only for oneself to receive such great knowledge.

In this respect, I can and will only tell the story of how I found the discus or how it found me.

Even that sounds crazy again, I know. But it always comes to me in the same way, because it was an encounter between the future and the past and that makes it so cyclical and non-linear and so almost impossible to tell about it linearly word for word.

I really don't remember much from that time, my brain was so overwhelmed and at times totally out of order.

To the facts. I do my best. Again, I practically have to jump in at some point, it's like it's a record with a whole track on it and I'm putting the needle up somewhere.

So I put the needle of my Discus story at the place when I started to work at the company Telelogic near Munich. It was in the spring of the year 2000 when my energy started to increase massively, again triggered by the already existing presence of the Venusian Omnec Onec in my life. At the same time there was another love story connected with it, a karmic one of course. But I don't want to digress, otherwise I will open too many circles – but this story with the musician, with whom I was in love in Landshut at that time for several years, it plays a role in the overall picture quite a bit, when it comes to the topic of love and heart and partnerships. But I'll come back to that later, for now it's just about the disc.

To organize and structure my energy and also because I needed money, I looked for a job. A simple office job. Obviously guided from above, I found it promptly – I had clearly sent out that I wanted a job that would pay me an hourly rate of 25 euros, that was not connected to a permanent job and that would give me a simple activity. I looked at that time on the Internet, which I already had in my apartment for a short time, although still mega slow and only temporary, but exactly the right job ad caught my eye. I called, made an appointment for an interview, drove there the next day and got the job!

Shortly after that, I started working and the job was perfect. I had a colleague who worked there as an assistant and was very nice, and a nice team, it was a simple sorting job. I was simply supposed to move paper from hanging files to standing files and label the new standing files accordingly. The job was limited to a few weeks because the company management thought that about four weeks would be enough for this sorting work, which was a realistic estimate.

Now I really liked it there, I felt comfortable and also had a lot of fun with myself and my colleagues, because my energy increased every day and I became more and more joyful and relaxed. People had so much fun with me, too, I think. Even though I worked well and reliably, I was not yet euphoric or otherwise super enthusiastic about the job.

After the sorting job was done, i.e. after the planned four weeks or so, I was even offered a permanent position, that's how good they thought I was. At that time, from my point of view, nothing stood in the way, because I still had nothing better to do, which would soon change, but at that time I agreed and signed the contract.

Soon after, the company moved to new, larger premises in the same area. I still performed a good service, because such a company move is a lot of work and I was very diligently integrated and helped with the packing and the process continued to work well. Then in the new rooms it happened and the sight of the Phaistos Disc and me met for the first time consciously.

In the corridor there was a copier, which I operated daily. And on the wall a few meters away, someone had hung up the company poster showing the Phaistos Disc with lettering and logo. I hadn't noticed that before, because the company I worked for was called Telelogic, but before that it was called S & P Media, and from that previous company there was still older advertising material that had the Phaistos Disc on it. These were postcards, brochures and also these large posters. I hadn't noticed all that in the old rooms because it was stored in cupboards there. But as a decorative element, and perhaps in honor of the company's founder, someone had hung the Phaistos Disc poster in the new rooms in the hallway near the copier.

Image 2: Poster with Phaistos Disc

And now it already starts to blur, because I don't know how many days I had been doing my copying work there clueless and in a good mood, until the contact between the poster and me happened.

Suddenly at that moment my third eye went into resonance with the center of the Phaistos Disc on the poster. I looked and from the flower of the discus stamped in the center of the day side, a ray of light streamed and opened my third eye in the center of my forehead. On the other hand, my third eye was already open anyway due to the months of energy uplift, and it went into resonance with the center of the Phaistos Disc. It was the moment of recognition and I knew only one thing immediately: I have to go to Crete!

It was totally clear to me that the Phaistos Disc had called me. I had only this one goal in mind, to see the Disc in the original on Crete. I think the information of its whereabouts was on the poster, so I knew where it was and where to go.

Now I knew that at that moment, but I was not yet loopy enough to just drop everything and get on a plane. I knew that there would still be a linear time between that moment and the real encounter with the real Discus in Heraklion. From my state of consciousness, I was in such a state that everything didn't matter in the sense of being perfectly guided and in order. I didn't know when I would travel nor with what means, because money I hardly had despite the job because of my lifestyle and my loose hand when it came to spending money. But I had zero doubts, I was already so high from my consciousness that I only knew, only felt, only saw, only sensed, only loved – all without fear, completely free of doubts and worries. I was completely trusting in God and letting things totally come to me and happen by themselves.

It didn't last long, how long, of course I don't remember, maybe a week, maybe another four weeks, in any case the day came when I provoked my own dismissal. I did it that way because I reacted more to energies and gestures than to words. My perception was already so extended and heightened, and so I perceived a gesture of my direct supervisor for me as a dismissal, although he did not mean and say it so directly.

It happened like this: I was going to have a day off, a Friday. Then suddenly work came in and my two direct bosses told me that I couldn't have the day off after all because we had to work. But I didn't accept that, because I thought I had worked enough in the last weeks and I had earned the day off. On a certain level it was pure self-love and self-respect, but it was also inner rebellion against the corporate system of exploitation that always finds some reason to keep sucking people dry instead of giving them the space and free time they need and also when they want it of their own accord. I had announced my day off quite some time before and therefore I did not see fit at all to give up my well-deserved day off just because of some sudden important order.

On the Thursday before the day off, Friday, one of the two bosses came to me again, because I had already said that I would definitely not come to work the next day, and got the confirmation from me again. And then he made a gesture like this; he said to me: I thought we were working together here! And I said: Yes, we do. That's what I meant, because for me it was absolutely important that I was respected for working well together and that my wishes for deserved leave were taken seriously. And then he clapped his hands once while turning away from me and said, "No, we don't."

And quite honestly – I in my extended, sensitive perception felt that was a dismissal! I felt like I was being terminated. I felt that from that point on, he was going to watch how he got rid of me, even though he didn't have the position of power to terminate me in real terms at that moment, he wasn't the top boss. Apart from that, the man and I didn't get along that well anyway, it went halfway, but we were never really on the same wavelength. And this gesture was the seal of the deal for me and I felt like I was being fired.

Well, and as it is in such a state of consciousness with the goal in mind to go to Crete to the Phaistos Disc, I felt totally happy and free! I just thought: Yes – I quit, yay! I am free!

On Monday, the real bosses and my colleagues, all except the one with the gesture, tried to persuade me to come back to the company. They really tried, even the highest boss personally called me and said that the direct supervisor could not dismiss me and that I should just come back to the office. But I was free and happy and didn't want to come back to the office.

So they really did terminate me and the matter was settled. I had found everything I needed there! HE had found me. HE had brought me into this company, so that I could find HIM. There was nothing more for me there!

Before my last day of work, I had pocketed a bunch of the Disc postcards and some of the brochures, I knew they wouldn't be needed anymore because the company name had changed. I still have some of these brochures and postcards today.

So was I now traveling directly to Crete?

No, it was still not yet time. After my end in the company Telelogic I somehow for some reason sneaked in the business of my friend at that time Martina. She had a liquid store and here again my memories blur – I don't remember exactly why I tried to get Martina to employ me in my loopy, convincing way, but she did! I had quite a wine phase at that time anyway and was drinking a lot of wine every day, and that also became more and more blatant. I drank wine partly then also during the day with her in front of the store, which of course attracted more and more negative attention. I was always in a good mood, but I was just strange in the eyes of others. I suppose a psychiatrist would have put the stamp "manic" on me. I also still tried to persuade Martina to give me money for my trip to Crete, so that I would find her good olive oil suppliers directly on site and help her to import directly and no longer through the franchise management. I found myself super smart and a genius with all my enhanced perceptual abilities and effervescent intuition and spiritual abilities.

I really had some kind of genius pill in me at the time – I was extremely fast in grasping ideas and thinking, and totally happy and deeply relaxed at the same time. I was serene, totally free, and completely in the flow of life.

This energy ultimately also lifted me out of my karmic bond with the musician, whom I had been following around like a puppy dog for four years at that time, according to the motto: "Looking for Love in all the wrong places". But I had to turn myself up so energetically, so to speak, so that I could finally let go of this attachment.

Martina then also definitely wanted to get rid of me and gave me the money for my trip to Crete. I don't remember exactly how much it was, it was exactly as much as I would need for the flight and with some housekeeping for a week's stay. Of course, I could not have known that the money would be used up after only four days, but even that did not matter to me, I was in God's trust and completely guided.

The day of my trip to Crete came closer and closer. Since I had a black, sweet tomcat in my apartment at that time, I asked Martina, as a last act of love for our fading friendship, to take care of the tomcat Odin, whom I had named after Omnec's uncle Odin, by the way, during my absence, which she did.

It was in September 2000 that I flew to Crete for the first time to see the Phaistos Disc in person. And it was not a normal trip, but an odyssey. The Gods of Greece were alive again. I was Artemis and a man I wanted to wrap around me was Apollo. A beautiful Swiss woman was Aphrodite and the Oracle of Delphi at the same time. I saw some other Gods in the form of people who were like funny play-mates for me on the game of my life.

The Ascended Master Hilarion, who has his etheric temple above Crete, became my best friend.

But one thing at a time, as far as I can from memory. The divine guidance is so perfect and that is exactly why it is so wonderful when I write down these memories now, because they remind me that everything is really perfectly guided, orchestrated and planned by a higher intelligence that is nothing but love.

For example, I remember the bus at the airport that took passengers to the plane. It was quite full. And there was a man with whom I casually struck up a conversation. He asked me where I was going. I said I didn't have a specific destination. He said the south was better for vacation than the north.

Okay, said then it was done. So I had decided that I wanted to go to the south of Crete.

The flight was calm and serene. Arrived in Heraklion, I took my light luggage, I traveled at that time really very easily with only few articles of clothing, there were still no technical devices, which I had to carry around and also books or other heavy stuff I did not have. Then I met the man again, he introduced himself to me as Klaus and said he was a cab driver in Munich and that he would pick up a rental car here, because he often travels to Crete and knows his way around and if he could take me with him to the south.

I thought that was great and I agreed immediately! So I had already secured my transport – all guided and unplanned, at least not planned by me. Also I did not have an overnight stay, of course, I knew that everything would turn out, I just wanted to drift and enjoy myself.

On the way to the south we stopped at a store and I supplied myself with Rezina and Sprite, which became my national drink for my stay in Crete and for the aftermath for a few months in Germany. Klaus and I then chatted during the car ride from Heraklion to the south of Crete, I did not yet know where we were going, and I told him that I had come to see the Phaistos Disc and visit it in the museum. Then Klaus told me that he knew a man, Fritz, who had written a book about the discus and that he lived very close to the place we were going to and where he could get me a room if I wanted.

I was beside myself with excitement! Really? A man who wrote a book about the discus? Now that's awesome! I knew I was on the right track!

When Klaus and I arrived in Pitsidia, that's the little town in the south not far from the sea, he quickly organized a room for me, I threw my backpack in there, and I jumped right into the hustle and bustle of people sitting outside at the many tables in the central square of Pitsidia, eating and drinking. It was wonderfully warm and there were lots of people there. I felt great! I had so arrived! So present, so at home, I felt really fantastic!

Somewhere I was sitting and eating and drinking when Klaus came to me and said, "Anja, the Fritz I told you about in the car and who wrote a book about the discus, he is here today!" I was totally happy and said, "Wow, really, would you please introduce us?" I was in such a royal mood, and everything I said and did had something Earthy and very polite about it. So Klaus accompanied me to meet Fritz, who was sitting at a table drinking wine with a couple of friends. I sat down with the little group and soon I asked Fritz straight out, "Fritz, what does the Phaistos Disc mean?" And Fritz said, "The disc contains the universal information." I beamed from all pores, looked Fritz deep in the eyes and just said, "I KNOW!"

And then we drank and at some point I fell unconscious into the bed, which I so do not remember at all.

During my time in Crete, I kept a diary. I kept it so I could track what day it was. I felt so multidimensional about it that I was involved in a timelessness and had no sense of time in a linear way at all. At least I was able to hang on to the diary. I wrote down everything I experienced in keywords, I thought to myself, if I would read it one day later, when my consciousness would have sunk again, which I already anticipated, then I would be able to call it up again, everything I had experienced.

Just like the discus! Also the discus contains words, symbols, and the one who has made it, knew that he would be able to recall and grasp it later when finding it again.

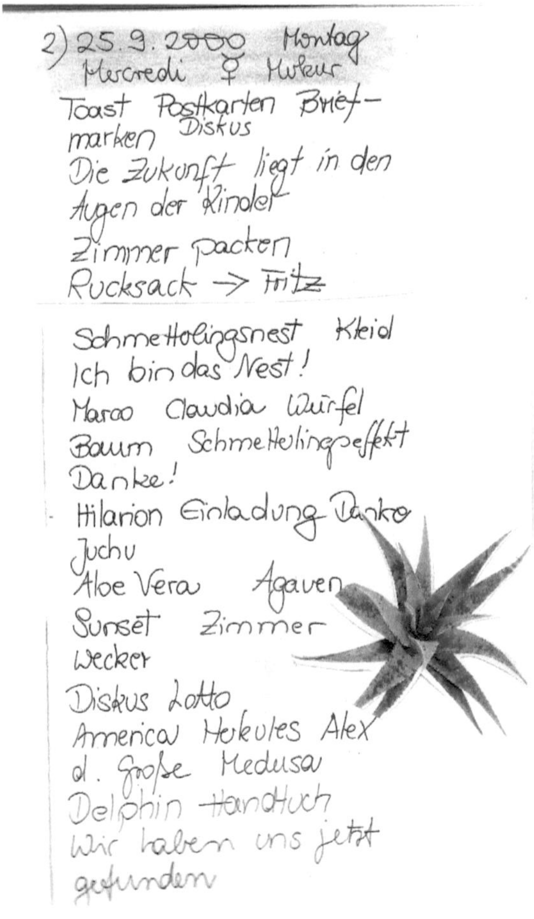

2) 25.9.2000 Montag
Mercredi ☿ Merkur
Toast Postkarten Brief-
marken Diskus
Die Zukunft liegt in den
Augen der Kinder
Zimmer packen
Rucksack → Fritz

Schmetterlingsnest Kleid
Ich bin das Nest!
Marco Claudia Würfel
Baum Schmetterlingseffekt
Danke!
Hilarion Einladung Danke
Juchu
Aloe Vera Agaven
Sunset Zimmer
Wecker
Diskus Lotto
America Herkules Alex
d. Große Medusa
Delphin Handtuch
Wir haben uns jetzt
gefunden

Image 3: Page from my Crete diary, 2000.

The next few days were all bright, fun, and extremely intense. I slept in a different room every day, was non-stop like a butterfly, talked to many people and drank wine, wine and wine. I think it was the very next day after I arrived in Pitsidia that I was blown away, namely when I somehow learned that the site of Phaistos, the place where the original disc was found in 1907, was only 6 kilometers away!

I was completely overwhelmed by the genius of divine guidance! Because I, my little Anja-me, did not know that! I had not planned the trip! I had only heard from Klaus that the south was better for vacation than the north and therefore I was ready to go with him to the south. But if you look at a map of Crete, you will see that the island has a west-east extension of 300 kilometers and that there is a lot of south where you can go on vacation! So it was a miracle that my spiritual guidance sent me exactly where Phaistos is located.

Thus I had a new goal! Apart from the museum in Heraklion, where the original discus was and is exhibited, I now absolutely wanted to go to Phaistos. And although there are only 6 kilometers between Pitsidia and Phaistos and the other place where I spent some nights is called Kalamaki at the sea, it was a little odyssey for me to find the way to Phaistos. In the end, it was only on the day before my departure, I think, or maybe sometime in the middle of my time in Crete, that my new friend Konstantin drove me by car to Phaistos and also accompanied me there as a kind of "male companion" – that is, in the sense of a courtly companion. I had also met Konstantin in Pitsidia during an evening. He was very sophisticated and spoke good German. He lived in Rhodes and was visiting Crete. He recognized my spirituality and therefore saw himself in a certain way also commissioned or at least inspired to drive me to Phaistos and to accompany me there. It was also a small pilgrimage for him to spend time with me, because I was just in a special mood – I was in an expanded state of consciousness and Konstantin felt that.

And now we are approaching the climax of my first trip to Crete, because, to anticipate and maybe you already suspect it: I did not make it to the museum to the real discus during my first trip! There is a good reason for this and I will tell you when I am through with my Phaistos story.

In Phaistos I arrived. I had never arrived in my life like I did in Phaistos. I was at home. As I walked across the central square, yes, walked, for I felt like royalty, I felt as if I were walking through my own living room. Heaven and Earth were united in me. I knew Phaistos was the stronghold of the queens. Years later, when I read the confirmation of my intuitive perception in Henry Miller's "The Colossus of Maroussi," I knew once again what inner truth felt like.

> *And I had the strong, intuitive feeling that Phaistos had been the women's castle of Minos' dynasty. The historian will smile, he knows better. But at that moment and from then on and forever, Phaistos becomes for me, despite all the evidence, despite all the logic, the residence of the queens.*[2]

Image 4: Phaistos in Southern Crete, the central square

Konstantin, my faithful companion, was thinking aloud to himself in the central square, "I wonder how King Minos found this magnificent place?" And suddenly a word fell into my completely empty head: HEUREKA! I pronounced it and asked Konstantin if he knew what it meant. He said it was pronounced in Greek like EVRIKA and it meant, "I

2 Henry Miller, The Colossus of Maroussi, RoRoRo 1999, p. 124 ff.

have found it!" So I said to Konstantin, "Evrika sounds like Erika. Erika is a woman's name. Minos didn't find this place, his wife did!" It was completely logical to me!

In Phaistos there is a café with a store. You can eat something there, drink good coffee and buy many nice souvenirs, of course also the Phaistos disc in all variations. When Konstantin and I took a break there and I ordered a sandwich while he snacked on green grapes, he asked me, "You are such a spiritual person. Why do you eat something so heavy and not the light fruit?" And I said to him, "Because I need that to ground. The fruit is too light for me now."

After that, I went for a little walk by myself and felt it's enough. It is high enough. Konstantin went alone behind the café and a little higher up the hill after I said to him, "You go ahead. I can't go any higher. I have reached my peak here."

I knew I meant that in more ways than one. I knew, from now on it can only go down again, but at this point I had reached my peak in consciousness and from the energy, more was not possible.

And that's exactly why I couldn't visit the original discus in the museum during my first trip to Crete. I knew later that it would have blown out the last bit of my mind if I had met the original in this perfect expansion. I had to and wanted to ground myself again, because this body is there for me to integrate all memories and the perfect light consciousness with mind into it and to radiate it and carry it on. If I had arrived physically, psychically or mentally in a state that would have been irreparable, then I could not fulfill my Soul plan.

Against this background it makes total sense that I was grounded again enough only two years later, namely exactly after my anti-day experience with the Prince of Darkness, to visit the Phaistos Disc in the original during my second trip to Crete, and then also as a child on the coat-tails of my parents, who had donated this trip to me as a small recreation and consolation after my hellish time at the side of the sorcerer at my request.

I still remember well this first time in the museum at the Discus. It was planned as a family trip with a rented car from the south of Crete, where my parents and I had a vacation apartment. For me, my parents have always been stressful when it came to dense areas, because there "you never find a parking space" (parents' original tone) and in case of doubt you just turn around and drive home. We had the same scenario during our visit to Heraklion, which is the capital of Crete and where cars are driving around and there is a lot of traffic and where you have to make sure that you can park your car if you don't have any parking spaces activated. And it was exactly this usual scenario that I faced when my father was about to drive back south with the car and me in the back without me going to my museum. That's when my blood welled up and I expressed clear resistance, even though I was still energetically weakened from the events two years earlier. By the way, I knew intuitively that the basic integration of my first two initiations would take between three and five years, by which I mean until I would be fit for work and halfway social again. That's pretty much how it was, because in mid-2004 I moved from Monchengladbach to Lake Constance and started a new job, in which I was able to slowly recover over the following years to the point where I was halfway able to get back into my body – even though I was about 20 kilos overweight. But this only as an insertion, in order to make clear that it was quite a feat of strength to oppose my father, who preferred not to find a parking place in the vicinity of the Phaistos Disc.

I sat on the back seat as a good child, my parents sat in the front and my father drove – and I said clearly from the back: "I'm not leaving this island as long as I haven't been to that museum!" My father not only heard that with his ears, but he knew I meant it, and suddenly a parking space was found. My parents didn't go to the museum, they didn't care. That was something minimally stupid for me, because it showed again that my parents had a certain role in my life, but being interested in my experiences and interests was not one of them.

So I went to the museum alone. I felt the discus already in the entrance. I was relatively grounded and super well off because of the hours before with my parents in the car I wasn't either, but the energy of the discus was crystal clear for me to feel – despite my energetic condensations. I felt its presence through vibrations of my chakras and through the vibrating, circling movement of my body, the Kundalini probably, I always feel this life energy as vibrations. It is this opening of the system, the life energy that flows, I always feel it in the vicinity of the discus and I can't really explain it to myself today that I react so extremely to it.

When I saw him in the flesh for the first time, when I stood in front of his glass vitrine in the museum, the reaction of my body-mind-Soul system was the strongest and I think, at the latest then, I also realized that I would not have been able to cope with seeing it two years earlier in my total awakening at that time, I really believe that my spiritual guidance prevented me from exposing myself to the proximity of the original.

But now, two years later, it did and I could still feel the energy strongly, but my fuses were not glowing because of it. I could perceive it and enjoy it and I stayed there as long as I wanted – my parents would already be waiting for me, that was clear.

In the years that followed, I went to Crete from time to time, and I always visited Phaistos and the Disc in the museum. Always I feel this energy there, but with each time over the last decades it became more adapted, my energy system slowly got used to the vibration and is integrating it, just as I am integrating the information from Omnec Onec and Dr. Raymond Keller, my two Venus teachers and friends.

It all feels like home, Soul, my Soul plan to remember who I really am and embody that knowledge with every cell of my being. It's also about reactivating the chakra system, opening up the locked DNA strands, it's about love, true, divine, high love, it's about the ticket home, ending the cycles and beginning new levels of experience, which in a sense are not new, but the return of the known, the true, the seemingly past, because in truth nothing has happened in the Soul level, in the higher dimensions is always Now.

Before I tell more about the woman from Venus, Omnec Onec, in the next chapter, I would like to insert a special feature here, which I have experienced only once in this physicality, namely the encounter with the Christ consciousness.

I can hardly put into words what happened there, but I will do my best.

I remember my apartment in Landshut during the peak of my second initiation around my first trip to Crete, when I wanted to go to the Phaistos Disc – and, as I told before, only arrived at Phaistos and at the Disc two years later.

In my apartment in Landshut there was a carpeting that I ruined during the time I lived there. I knew intuitively that I would soon be moving out of there, and I also knew that the carpeting would be ruined anyway, and that I didn't need to pay any attention to it. In retrospect, with my usual common sense, I don't know what got into me – maybe the carpeting had some damage before I moved in anyway, and so I felt a green light to let my messy behavior finish it off.

In other words, I caused burn marks, because I still smoked, I poured out the one or other glass of wine, I drank quite a lot at that time, preferably red wine – which already contains a hint to the Christ experience – and I let my burning candle spill its wax. I also had a pottery chalice, I don't remember where I got it, but it was blue-green and really beautiful, a real ritual chalice, from which I always drank my wine when I was at home.

I had a beautiful candlestick with a red candle. I remember that I always left this candle burning, even when I left the apartment. For me it was pure trust in God, I just knew that Christ was at home with me – the constant burning of the candle was a kind of ritual for me. Yes, exactly what was going on inside me I can hardly remember, but I particularly remember an experience of feeling the Holy Spirit enter me through my crown center. I felt him like a dove and there I also had the realization about why so often the white dove is depicted as a symbol over representations of saints. I thought, this is what it really feels like! It was an energetic white dove that went over my crown chakra into my heart and has been there ever since. I never experienced anything like that again, it was just at that one time.

When I was in Crete, I remember, I had a phase of Soul liberation – there I was running like a Duracell bunny through the cemetery of Pitsidia. I felt like a beacon, my heart was on fire and I had tremendous energy in my body, pure life energy flowing through me as I walked through that cemetery and touched all the graves with my light of consciousness, that is, with my energy, some gravestones I touched also physically, and liberated the ignorant Souls that were still trapped there because of false teaching and false beliefs.

For me it was an act of love for Jesus Christ, because from Omnec and her Christ story I knew that Christ was held in a certain frequency – if it is still like that today, I am not sure – maybe it is not like that anymore, but at that time I felt inside this mission to at least do my little bit to help some Souls to find the truth and the light and not to stick to Christ any longer and be stuck in some artificial heaven.

Omnec told it in such a way that the established churches were built to keep Jesus Christ stuck in a realm of the causal plane and thus prevent him from being able to evolve, when quite a lot of Souls on Earth follow a false belief and spend their lives in the name of Jesus Christ and do everything in his name, that they impose everything on him, which in truth is their own thing. But somehow it was probably so, at least this information was transmitted to Omnec in this way and so she passed it on then, that Christ would not be free as long as these church structures exist and many people hold on to the erroneous belief that Christ died for their sins and that there is a hell and really believe, that they need the church as a mediator to God, that is simply not true and Jesus exemplified and explained to people that through him, that is, through the heart, through love, one finds God and that this is open to all people because all people are children of God and not just some. The one was only the example, the pioneer, the symbol, he exemplified it and for thousands of years his words and teachings have been misused and misinterpreted.

Omnec tells in her autobiography part 2 "Angels Don't Cry" about her experiences as a child in the 50's and 60's, where there was still a lot of religious fanaticism and also racial judgement and said so nice childishly that she had never fully understood this "business with the blood of Christ" and that all this did not make sense to her. What she has witnessed as a child on Earth and what so many adults unfortunately believe in through the established control system and pass it on to their descendants for thousands of years.

Anyway, I made my modest contribution in that I helped at least a few stuck Souls in a Cretan cemetery into the light and that to the joy of the Christ presence in my heart, which was just super present at that time.

Triggered by Omnec and by the Phaistos Disc, my heart and Third Eye were wide open to Divine Love and to the remembrance of my true self as a Being of Light. Twenty-two years later, I experienced an upgrade in love. This third initiation was a heart opening in another dimension. It opened my consciousness to love at eye level and hand in hand with my divine Beloved, and at the same time renewed and deepened into God Presence. Keywords like Hieros Gamos, Unio Mystica and Holy Trinity[3] may give an impression.

3 The Hieros Gamos is the marriage of opposites, of inside and outside, the inner Divine-Masculine and Divine-Feminine, the mind and heart. Unio Mystica is the mystical union with the Divine. Hieros Gamos and Unio Mystica are intertwined. They are not necessarily experienced in a sequential order, are not always permanent, and must be cultivated as a practice. By Holy Trinity is classically meant the Holy Trinity - that is, God the Father, God the Son, and the Holy Spirit. Personally, by Trinity I also mean the triad - God - Divine-Male - Divine-Female aspect of the Soul.

Phaistos Disc. Archaeological Museum, Crete, Greece. Photos from Anja Schäfer venus-spirit.com

Image 5: Both sides of the Phaistos Disc.

Chapter 7 – Omnec Onec from Venus

Imagination is the key to creation.

– Omnec Onec

Which came first – the hen or the egg? The Omnec or the Anja? In this life it appears to be her, and yet – as is the nature of the cyclic – connections gradually reveal themselves, so that the answer as to what connection she and I in reality have is no longer quite so simple.

Especially since more and more people looked at Omnec's book, then looked at me, and then looked at the book again, and then asked me: Is that YOU? I began to wonder what was going on. Because Omnec and I really have almost nothing in common on the outside! She is super blond, I am brown-haired. She is very slim, I am rather normal with the tendency to be a little overweight. Omnec has green eyes, I have brown ones.

These oddities happened from time to time already in the middle time of our joint activity, I mean the period around the year 2010. It became even more conspicuous in the year 2022, when also Robert Potter, Venus contactee, long-time fan of Omnec and organizer of the Mount Shasta summer conferences, and Dr. Raymond Keller, Historian of the Venusians and up to now author of seven books about Venus, especially in conversations, interviews and also publicly again and again called me Omnec or spoke about me and did not say Anja, but Omnec.

Of course, that was always amusing for me and if people caught on, for them as well. But it is simply a small phenomenon, which can be explained most simply by the fact that Omnec's and my energies are very similar and aligning more and more.

Image 6: Omnec Onec. Cover photo from "The Venusian Trilogy".

In 2022, when Dr. Raymond Keller, who is also known as Cosmic Ray and whom I simply call Ray, was with me in Germany, he even SAW on at least one occasion that Omnec's energy field was becoming more and more like a kind of cloak over me and merging with mine.

It is quite possible that Omnec and I are at least Soul sisters, that we belong to one Soul family. What other reasons there are for our close, lifelong interaction will still be revealed. It is easiest for me to stick to the facts, because they are easy to tell. What else may be behind it mentally and spiritually and what is relevant for you in it, that is between the lines.

I am writing this book, as indicated in the beginning, both for myself to complete cycles and for you and the Earth as my gift, as my inheritance or one of my heirlooms, because I have so much more to give and share. In fact, I have written a lot, I just haven't published anything of my own yet. During my dark period at Bernold's company, I also wrote daily, but I never revised that, let alone published it. I was also alone for two weeks one time on Crete and wrote daily. From this came a book manuscript, which still lies in a drawer. It's not all meant to be shared either. Sometimes writing is also simply a kind of mental hygiene and helps to process what I have experienced.

So far, my main task has been to serve and assist others and to promote THEIR works.

But – and here we are back to the cyclic nature – I feel that now it is about a kind of reversal and that I should also give birth to my own information and content. That doesn't mean I'm going to stop supporting Omnec and Ray and others I love and value in their work. But something inside me says that it's now also about expressing my own experiences and insights – and even if it's just a kind of dare for myself to put myself out there more. What I share is not just accumulated knowledge from decades of research, reading many books, watching numerous videos, listening to lectures and learning in seminars and trainings. That's not the gist of it. Otherwise I could just write a scientific paper here, LINEAR even, and put facts together and maybe add my own two cents or draw conclusions, whatever, kind of like writing a doctoral thesis.

My life is deeper than that – it's not about accumulated knowledge. I have had wonderful spiritual experiences, enlightening experiences, and have been able to transform some knowledge into wisdom. I'm like a little alchemical cauldron, continuously bubbling away, turning more and more information into gold.

The only people who have known me all my life and with whom I am still connected are my parents. I wonder what they noticed about my development so far? That's hard to say, and it would be hard for them to tell me, because for them I'm simply Anja, their only child. But one thing is for sure: they are proud of me and happy that I am the way I am, even if they don't fully understand me. If I had remained unconscious and remained in separation consciousness, we probably would have gone our separate ways at one point in our lives and not had so much love and closeness with each other. This connection between me and my parents is possible in the way it is only because Omnec Onec brought me the blessing of unconditional love and acceptance. Through Omnec's presence in my life and through her teachings and love, I was elevated to another level of being, and only from that depth or height, however you may see it, have I since been able to unconditionally accept my parents as they are, that is, without holding grudges in the past, without resenting anything, without expecting anything from them, without being disappointed or anything like that, which most often causes conflict between people or perpetuates separation. Through Omnec and the love she transmitted to me, I was able to forgive my parents for everything they seemed to have done to me or for what they failed to do – simply out of their own unconsciousness.

From my perspective, my parents were and have been perfect for me and my development, but without an expanded heart perspective, I could never have seen it that way. I would have remained in the consciousness of seeming unlovable and being wrong here, I think. And that would have really broken my parents' hearts, because for them it was not a part of their life plans to set out on their own on the spiritual search for God and divine love – that was my job, so to speak. In this respect it was up to me to include my parents in MY heart, in my expanded, loving heart and to take them as they are. They would not have succeeded with me the other way around, because until today in their old age – both are over 80, now as I type these lines – they have not decided for awakening. And by awakening I mean at this point the opening of themselves to the God-presence within themselves, to truth, to divine love. And that's perfectly fine the way it is, and maybe I'm looking at it all wrong. In any case, my parents did their jobs brilliantly and fulfilled the Soul contract with me. They gave me my body and my home – physically. They always provided me with everything I needed – physically, materially, and the bare necessities emotionally and mentally. That was the deal between us. They gave me a stable set of parents – they have been married to each other for over sixty years and never spent a minute without each other, especially since my father stopped driving out, which is what they called his job. My father was a long-distance driver for a furniture company and went out every Monday during my childhood and teenage years and then usually came home again on Friday. But I don't want to tell you everything about my parents and my childhood – it should be enough up to this point – the main point is that Omnec and the bringing of love had an impact on several levels – and the connection between me and my parents was one of them.

I have told the story of my coming together with Omnec a few times, both in my and Omnec's book "Simply Wisdom and Love – Venusian Spirituality" and in several interviews and videos.

But maybe you don't even know who Omnec is! If that's the case, then I'd like to give you a brief insight here: Omnec Onec is, as far as is known, the only person in the world who was brought to Earth as a child with her own manifested body. So she is a real extraterrestrial and from my point of view the only person who can truly say that she came from Venus.

If you've never heard that before, but so far you've read my book up to this point, then you'll probably be able to handle it. I guess, otherwise you wouldn't want to listen to me anyway, because everything I share here is on a high spiritual level and includes spiritual knowledge in itself, to which many people on Earth don't have conscious access yet – but this is precisely what should and may and will change and that's exactly why people like Omnec and me are here and tell our stories. We tell our stories and share our knowledge to reach hearts, to expand consciousness and to offer perspectives that go far beyond the usual learned and programmed "knowledge". It's also about finding Soulmates, because when we show up and tell and publish our stories, we find each other more easily.

We are all connected and that's why we tell our stories not only for others, but also for ourselves. That's exactly why I'm writing all of this down, so that it's out of me, because I know I'm making room for something new, and because I know that by writing it out and revising it, I'm reflecting on myself and in turn internalizing and processing more of all of it than I would if I continued to keep it all inside of me, or keep it all inside of me forever. And who knows – maybe you'll be the one who contacts me because of this book and we'll remember each other.

Omnec also told her life story and went public because it was connected to her mission and her Soul mission and also for herself to complete her reincarnation cycles. It was destined for her, it was her mission to share her knowledge with people and at the same time, through the reflux and the restored connections with soulmates, to stimulate their consciousness to awaken. And this return flow of energies and people's love perfects Omnec's existence, so that one day she will ascend to the higher dimensions as a Soul. From my point of view, she has already ascended, she is only physically present and I don't know if she will eventually take her body with her or leave it behind like a skin she doesn't need anymore. Probably the latter, but we will see that when the day of transformation comes.

The knowledge about the existence of the Soul, the creative source, which we can also call God or Mother-Father-God, the knowledge about reincarnations, about the true history of the Earth and its colonizations, the knowledge about higher dimensions, linear and cyclic time and the knowledge about extraterrestrial life belong here.

I suppose people who still classify everything I just listed as science fiction or fantasy won't read these words anyway. But in truth I write down my story also for them, because even if they don't read it consciously, I upload this energy as frequencies into the morphogenetic field of the Earth and from there they connect with equal forces, and all this together forms a pool of information, which in dreams, during out-of-body experiences or through seemingly random encounters or conspicuousness ultimately reaches many more embodied Souls than we can keep track of.

The other way round it is also true, that means that I also call up memories from this field and feel inspired to now sit here at my laptop in Turkey and release all that is in me and give it away to the out-side.

It is probably even the case – or certainly it is – that my Soul, that is, my true self, my Higher Self, has planned it so that I sit here at this time, precisely UM to make certain inner connections and to write this book.

When I think about it and look at it in this way, I even have to complete it and publish it, because there must be a good reason for it, which I cannot yet fully grasp. Whether it's just the reason I took as a hook at the beginning of this book, my conscious mind doesn't know yet.

You remember? I started writing because while I was walking the day before I left here, I was thinking about what open cycles I have left in my life and what I would do if I knew I was leaving this body in a few months. I'm guessing that I really won't "die" yet, but I really can't know. Maybe it is also about a total transformation, which I really wish for. I wish that from now on my life turns inward, that I stabilize my Soul consciousness and that I really AM and have more than a constant 50% of the God connection. This sounds modest and that's how I mean it, because I can't undertake or promise myself that I will stay in the perfect state of enlightenment non-stop. I truly believe – both from my own experience and from the experiences of others – that enlightenment does not mean permanently dwelling in a holy state à la Buddha under the Bodhi tree from a sudden moment.

Many people associate enlightenment with a certain idea. I know only one thing: only an enlightened person recognizes an enlightened person. So if you are reading these words, for example, but have never had an enlightenment experience, then it may well be that you find all this exciting, interesting or even amusing – or, on the contrary, totally detached, nonsensical and superfluous. But you may not perceive anything "enlightened" in it. However, just imagine, there is something "enlightened" in it and some spark jumps over to you, without you consciously noticing it, and lights a little fire that spreads in you over the course of the next time, months or years. And all of a sudden, sometime in the so-called future, you experience something and suddenly you know what enlightenment is. You suddenly have a lamp go on, or your heart opens, or some combination of symptoms, or you experience coincidences and conspicuities, synchronicities, a miracle, God is very creative there, there are no limits to the radius of experience.

And then maybe you think back to this book, maybe you still have it buried somewhere on a shelf, or you suddenly look for it and realize that you gave it away or threw it away a long time ago and think: Man, I would really like to take a look at it again – Anja has described exactly what I am experiencing now!

Yes, and you know what? Your own Soul controls that, exactly all that. Your enlightened self in the apparent future is also present in your present self, which reads these lines, and has caused you to read this book.

Yes, God is brilliant! God is definitely the perfect in the perfect. It is only in the lower dimensions that IT expresses itself through the imperfect in the perfect, because here we are in duality and have our experiences through the contrast and the seemingly imperfect.

Oh my goodness – I still have not told how I got to know Omnec now, but now really!

I will keep the story reasonably linear, because otherwise I draw again loud circles and circles and open many doors, which I must close again somewhere, so that you do not lose the thread.

Omnec Onec was living in the USA when her autobiography "From Venus I Came" was first published in 1991. This began her public work and one day she spoke at a UFO conference. A German was there, recognized her authenticity and invited her to Germany. Soon Omnec traveled to Germany and not long after her book was published in German under the title "Ich kam von der Venus". This marked the beginning of Omnec's public time in the German-speaking world, and from then on she returned to the U.S. only privately – otherwise her entire work was focused on Germany, Switzerland and Austria.

I will try to fathom the reasons for this in a later chapter on the Venus-Germany connection.

But one thing is for sure – I myself was born in Germany and it was destined for me and Omnec to meet so that I would become her student, her assistant and ultimately – and it seems I am standing in front of this door right now – a kind of spiritual successor.

It was around 1993 or 1994 when I "accidentally" turned on the television and saw her there on a talk show. She caught my attention right away because she was so beautiful, so calm, and spoke such wonderful words such as "Imagination is the Key to Creation." Never before had I seen or heard a person on television who made such an impression on me. Omnec immediately struck me as truthful, and I was also fascinated by her name and the title of the book, "From Venus I Came."

A seed was planted.

A few years later at the beginning of 1996 – my spiritual guidance had threaded all this perfectly – I moved from my hometown Berlin to Landshut in Bavaria. My old environment in Berlin had crumbled due to my increasingly extreme interests in esotericism and astrology, and I no longer had any friends. My parents also didn't know what to do with me and were in any case quite sad and desperate about the fact that I just couldn't find a man, that I didn't want to follow a normal professional path and that I was anyway just different from what they had wanted from their only daughter at that time. But they also had the inner mandate to leave me free and not to overly control or manipulate me. That was difficult for them, but they had each other and they just knew from within that they could not fight against my path in life, they just knew intuitively that they had to make me and let me go and that they were still my parents and had to keep an eye on me, especially materially and financially and to be a stable, Earthly parent for me, because the spiritual, emotional, mental and intellectual were not their fields of responsibility. This is absolutely value-free. Nothing here is better or worse than another.

Through an astrology seminar I had met Martina from Landshut and through her I got into a new environment in Landshut, into the circle of friends around Martina: the "girls". For them I was exotic and interesting. I was the youngest among them, was hardcore esoteric and from Berlin, which radiated a special charm for many. For a while they had accepted me into their circle, but after the beginning of my time with Omnec and the following expansions of consciousness, which for the normal fellow citizen seemed like pure "she has lost her mind", this circle also crumbled apart again and never reformed. Since I left Landshut at the end of 2000, I have never had any contact with any of them again.

But when everything was still fresh and exciting, Martina lent me money so that I could fulfill my heart's desire at that time: To open an esoteric bookstore. On February 1, 1997, I opened Lichtblick, the first esoteric bookstore in deeply Catholic Landshut, in the city with the highest brick church tower in the world, which speaks for itself.

Only an immigrant could organize something like that, and of course that was a good thing. Somebody has to start bringing fresh wind into the walled-up heads everywhere. Now I was not destined to lead this business there into some kind of material success and permanence – it was ultimately destined to give a push into the encrusted energy of the people and the field there. There was also a karmic reason related to a man I met again in my business and with whom I had an open cycle that I completed there.

But the most far-reaching and relevant reason for opening the Lichtblick in Landshut was that I met Omnec Onec there.

There she comes from Venus to Earth, lands in Tibet to get used to her body, is brought to the USA, where she lives among the people unrecognized for some decades, writes her autobiography, is brought to Germany, where she enters into a cooperation with a music producer and manager and with whom she then floats in his big Mercedes from Oldenburg to Landshut into my bookstore sometime in 1997 or 1998.

That's quite a trip, isn't it?

How did it come about, you might ask? It was because I was buying a huge pile of books for the Lichtblick's initial stocking, which I really enjoyed. It was only then that I remembered Omnec Onec's book, "From Venus I Came," which she had presented on that television program a few years earlier. I ordered this book for myself privately and started reading it in the opening stages of my business. I was more captivated and moved by this story than I had ever been by reading any other book in my life. I felt the love, the truth, and I felt something like "home." I just knew all of a sudden that I have the freedom to believe what I like and even if it is just fantasy, I told myself, then I choose to believe in that fantasy. So powerful had Omnec's words "Imagination is the Key to Creation" been on me! Because that key phrase alone gave me the self-empowerment to create my world the way I want to imagine it.

And when I read Omnec's descriptions of the astral plane of Venus with all the wonderful houses and temples and masters and the fantastic technology, when I learned for the first time about the colonization of our solar system and about the laws of the Supreme Deity and about the fact that the Venusians were also once a physical people and that they were raised as a society to a higher vibrational frequency and how it came about that they received this blessing from the Supreme Deity, when I read all this for the first time, I just knew: YES! This is true. I decide that this is true because it feels good and right in me.

Immediately afterwards, I ordered the second book by Omnec available at that time, entitled "Handbook of Venusian Spirituality" and my impression deepened, so much so that I felt: I have to see this woman!

When this decision was made, and I thought I would travel everywhere to hear a lecture with her, I contacted the publisher at that time, who kindly referred me to Omnec's music producer and then manager Wulf. When I called Wulf and told him that I would like to see Omnec in person and that I had a store in Landshut, he told me that she was with him right now and that they could come to me in Landshut if I would organize something for Omnec.

I could hardly believe my ears. Of course I was immediately on fire and spontaneously agreed! I was superhumanly happy and hopped around my store after the show: Omnec Onec is coming to Landshut – Omnec Onec is coming to Landshut!

The date was set for already three weeks later and Wulf sent me some kind of contract and a bunch of posters. Of course I really would have signed anything, I just felt and knew that this is all right and mega super awesome. Immediately I planned like crazy, organized a room for the talk, hotel rooms for them, taped posters and made an appointment with regional TV. I really told absolutely EVERYONE that Omnec Onec, the woman from Venus, was coming to Landshut and managed to have about 80 people sitting in the hotel room on the evening of the lecture, waiting dutifully for the arrival of the Venusian woman who, as usual, was much too late.

Yes, the Earthly time calculation was never Omnec's strength and since she and Wulf had to cope with a rather long car ride from Oldenburg to Landshut and the two of them would have had to leave very early in the morning, they finally arrived almost two hours late.

And as I was then – unconscious, unredeemed, full of euphoria and on my way to become a spiritual finder myself – I was simply a nervous wreck. I was still far too unrelaxed and full of anxiety, so I couldn't even entertain or reassure the waiting people or somehow even speak in a soothing tone to them. None of that worked at all – I was just stressed out.

Now I am just a bit confused with my own storytelling, because from my memory I did see Omnec and Wulf the first time in front of my store and not in the hotel – but it doesn't matter. Something got mixed up here, but the only thing that matters is that the first time I saw Omnec, I saw her like a holy angel. She was dressed all in white with tall white boots. She was all friendly and calm and the first thing she had to do was go to the bathroom. Yikes, a woman from Venus wants to use my little bathroom in the back of the store?!

Yes, at first I really put her on a pedestal – she was so special to me and I felt so unworthy and also extremely grateful and humble. I experienced feelings that I didn't know I had in this life; and through Omnec's presence I soon experienced my first expansion of consciousness and my first opening of the heart. I'll tell you about that in one of the next chapters in connection with the spiritual initiations I've experienced so far.

In-Drop No. 1: Experiences with the Venusian Omnec Onec

As an "in-drop" – this is a spontaneous word creation by which I mean the "dripping" of a thought-form into this book, I am inserting here my article about my early days with Omnec Onec as I casually wrote it at the beginning of the year 2000 and as it was printed in the German newspaper "The Other Reality" at that time.

Although in comparison to what I write now 23 years later in this book, especially in the first part of the article, some things are repeated, I decided to leave the original text completely as it is, because I think that in the overall impression you can still well feel my joy and initial euphoria between the lines.

Image 7: In service as Omnec's translator. 2003

A small recommendation for you: If you don't feel like reading a repetition now, feel free to take a mental breather, let your thoughts drip down into your heart, read on in Chapter 8, and come back here later.

"My girlfriend comes from Venus" – Article from the year 2000

Spirituelle Persönlichkeit

1. März 2000

Meine Freundin kommt von der Venus

Erlebnisse mit der Venusierin Omnec Onec

von Anja Schäfer

OMNEC ONEC

Auf dem Venus-Dance-Workshop im Sommer 1999
Anja Schäfer links, Omnec Onec rechts

Wer ist Omnec Onec?

Omnec Onec kam im Jahre 1955 mit einem Raumschiff von der Venus. Sie lebte bis dahin auf der Astralebene der Venus, die physische Ebene ist dort schon seit sehr langer Zeit nicht mehr bewohnt. Ein Mutterschiff brachte das UFO in Erdnähe, von wo aus sie zunächst in ein abgelegenes Kloster in Tibet gebracht wurde. Sie hatte sich auf der Venus den siebenjährigen Körper eines kleinen Mädchens manifestiert, an den sie sich erst einmal gewöhnen mußte. Omnec verbrachte etwa ein Jahr in Tibet, wo sie die englische Sprache lernte und sich mit den Funktionen des physischen Körpers vertraut machte. Als sie dann bereit war und gut genug für ihr Leben auf der Erde vorbereitet war, wurde sie wieder mit einem UFO in die USA gebracht. Zu jenem Zeitpunkt war das gleichaltrige Mädchen Sheila Gibson gerade mit einem Bus auf dem Weg zu ihrer Großmutter, bei der sie ein Jahr bleiben sollte. Dieser Bus geriet in ein Unglück, wobei Sheila ums Leben kam. Ihr Körper verbrannte. Omnec war dort und nahm dann den Platz von Sheila ein. Auf diese Weise kam sie in ihre amerikanische Familie.

Warum ist sie hier?

Die Erde befindet sich in einer tiefgreifenden Transformation. Die Schwingungs- und damit Bewußtseinserhöhung des gesamten Planeten ist ein laufender Prozeß, der damit begann, daß im Jahr 1993 die alten, zum Teil verborgenen, Tempelanlagen reaktiviert wurden. Das Bewußtsein der Menschen auf der Erde ist vergleichsweise niedrig und muß sich erweitern, damit die Erde sich nicht selbst zerstört, so wie dies andere Zivilisationen vor uns schon getan haben. Außerirdische Besucher haben schon seit langer Zeit Kontakt mit unseren Regierungen aufgenommen, aber es war keine Zusammenarbeit möglich, da die herrschenden Machthaber dieser Erde ihre Machtstellungen nicht verlieren möchten. Diese Macht wird in erster Linie durch Angstmache und Kontrolle über die Menschen aufrecht erhalten. Da all diese Versuche scheiterten, wurde ein Kind auf die Erde geschickt, damit es in unserer Gesellschaft aufwächst und all die Schwierigkeiten selber erlebt, die bei uns jeder Mensch erfährt und später dann von „unten", das heißt in direktem Kontakt mit kleinen Gruppen von Menschen, spirituelles Wissen weitergibt.

Seit einigen Jahren nun reist Omnec vorrangig durch Deutschland, Österreich und die Schweiz, um ihre Zuhörer mit Wissen zu versorgen. Sie erzählt die verloren gegangene Geschichte unseres Planeten und zeigt die Gründe auf, warum wir heute da sind, wo wir sind, welche Entwicklung uns bevorsteht und was jeder Einzelne von uns tun kann, um diese Entwicklung zu unterstützen.

© 2000 Anja Schäfer | www.venus-spirit.com

Image 8: First article about experiences with Omnec Onec.

For the first time I saw Omnec Onec on a talk show on television. I have never watched much television, certainly not on a regular basis, so it was a miracle that I turned on the TV at the very moment she was sitting there. Her voice, her appearance, her name and what she was talking about had all caught my full attention. I sat spellbound in front of the TV screen and was particularly taken with her statement, "Imagination is the key to creation. (Imagination is the key to creation)." She spoke in a way that triggered in me the feeling that she was speaking truths. I then "forgot" the whole experience, but somewhere deep inside me at that moment a seed was planted that took a few years to come up. For it was not until many years later that I obtained her book through my former esoteric bookstore in Landshut. When I then read the book, I was again deeply touched in the same way as when we first "met" via the TV screen. I felt longing and compassion and thought to myself how wonderful it would be if it were all true what Omnec writes in her book about her time on the astral plane of Venus. Would it really be true that life exists there, that you can manifest there with your mind power according to your wishes and ideas, that you can simply teleport yourself to other places and also transform into other forms at will? And where else is there life everywhere, what else is there to discover that I don't have a clue about yet? Wow, I thought, and then all the temples of learning. For years I was here looking for a study that would teach me what I was interested in. Then I gave it up because I realized that on Earth, in our social system, I would not find the things that excite me. Deep down, I felt that this autobiography was more than just a novel. After all, I had seen Omnec on TV for a few minutes before and knew that she was telling her story, just as I tell that I was born in Berlin, have no siblings and my parents now live in Spain. Very "normal" simple.

It took another year until I ordered her second book "Handbook of Venusian Spirituality". At that time Omnec already seemed to me to be a friend I would like to see (again) in person. So I called the Omega publishing house in Düsseldorf and was referred to Omnec's organizer and music producer Wulf Wemmje in Oldenburg, whom I also reached promptly. I just wanted to know when Omnec would be back in Germany so that I could go to one of their lectures. So I learned from Wulf that they were not only there, but that they also had a date free and could hold a lecture and a seminar directly at my place in Landshut. Three weeks later already. Of course I accepted the offer, and when I hung up the phone, I jumped around my whole store like a rubber ball and cheered "Omnec is coming to Landshut ¬ Omnec is coming to Landshut ¬ Yay!!!". Then I called all my friends and acquaintances, because none of them had ever seen me so joyful, and I wanted to not only inform them about this insane event, but also show them how much I can be happy. I was in this total high for over two hours, then I slowly came back down and right into the stress, because I really didn't have much time to announce and promote this weekend with Omnec. So I was whirling around, pasting posters, creating flyers, placing ads, making an appointment on regional TV, and mailing letters to customers. As the hour of their arrival approached, I was very excited. By now I have become accustomed to Omnec often showing up at the last minute, and so it was that evening of our first meeting. She doesn't "believe" in the man-made concept of time and has a hard time with it. Wulf and she arrived about 10 minutes before the scheduled live interview on Landshut Regional Television. As often in first encounters Omnec seemed a bit cool and distant to me, meanwhile I know that she is one of the most warm-hearted compassionate people walking around on this Earth. She doesn't just express her love by grinning incessantly like a honey-cake horse, no, she behaves completely naturally. Like many other people, I was simply overwhelmed by her presence and had to slowly get used to everything. After all, she is from Venus, you don't meet a person like that every day. My heart never had any doubts about the truth of her story, my mind of course had its problems with it at the beginning. But it also gets used to it, I have noticed. My mind never demanded any "proof" from her, just like a typical scientist once pulled a lighter out of his pocket in a TV show in the USA and wanted to burn Omnec with it. He thought that since she was from hot

Venus, she must be able to withstand heat just fine. He did not understand that Omnec comes from the astral plane of Venus, it was simply beyond his imagination.

Image 9: Omnec and Anja at a Venus Dance Workshop, 1999.

The heart now wears the pants in me, that is one of the many things I have learned through Omnec. The first thing Omnec wanted to do after arriving in Landshut was to go to the bathroom. Oh dear, I thought, my little loo in the back of the store, hopefully she won't mind and oops, she has to go to the toilet too, well, logical really, she's human. Many months later, when we were already very familiar with each other and were in the bathroom together, I remarked "Wow, you even have a belly button" to which she said "Yeah right, otherwise they would put me in a circus!". My mind did not understand that, of course, where she got the belly button, if she was not born on Earth. It's ingenious, I thought, that they can manifest such real human bodies on Venus, which differ from ours only in little things, but which can't be seen. Omnec, Wulf and I then went to the regional radio station, which had its studio only five minutes away from my store, and the two had to go in front of the camera immediately. Sure, at the last minute, it's often like that. One big lesson you learn with Omnec is to stay calm and collected even in the most impossible, stressful, nerve-wracking situations. Omnec and Wulf had that calm, I was behind the camera shaking with excitement. Stupid, I think to myself today, by now I am even able to be in front of the camera myself without dying of inner overload. I have never cared about getting into such situations where I am visible to the public. But those who really get involved with Omnec come up against their deepest fears and insecurities in order to overcome them. Because she has this gift of putting you in these situations, and it always looks like a coincidence. She doesn't plan it, I know that. Planning is a matter of the mind. Omnec is exceedingly intelligent, but I don't perceive her as being guided by reason in any way, on the contrary, she is "astral-logical" (the combination of feelings and logic is in itself illogical), irrational, and follows nothing but her feelings and intuition. So she gave her first lecture in medieval, Catholic Landshut, to which about 50 people came. Then for the workshop, about 12 came, all of whom had decided to attend the evening of the lecture. This is also almost a rule, that many people decide to participate in the seminar at very short notice. The ways people find Omnec are also as varied as the people themselves. One woman found a flyer while walking in the autumn leaves, a couple had independently heard the only two radio announcements and felt they were being addressed together, often people dream about Omnec and occasionally it is the children who see Omnec on a poster and drag their mother or father to the talk. Then during the workshop I slowly calmed down a bit and Omnec and I exchanged glances. That's when I really felt her and knew that I just loved her. Just like that. When we said goodbye after the weekend, I would not have guessed; that I would see her again at all.

I thought to myself that Landshut was just one size too small for her and that she would certainly not come there again. But I was wrong. She and Wulf came back half a year later. Then on Sunday, before the workshop began, I summoned up all my courage, overcame another hurdle and asked Omnec if she would like to stay an extra night and accompany me to a concert by the Boogie Woogie Quartet in the evening. They are four fantastic pianists on two pianos who are a lot of fun. Then in the afternoon she said yes. I was again out of my mind and was really looking forward to the evening. We then drove with a friend in a Fiat Panda without heating through snow flurries at snail's pace to Murnau, two hours away. I was stressed because I knew that we would not reach the second half of the concert at the earliest because we were way too late due to the late end of the seminar. Again, I was the only one who was nervous. As I had suspected, we got there just at the end of the first half and went to the restrooms first. On the way down to the lower floor was a large patio window and behind it was a large plant, some kind of agave. And there were two orange dots stuck on the window. Normally I would never have noticed that. Omnec said, "Look at this monster!" and then I saw what she saw. The two dots on the disk became two eyes and the shape of the plant became a many-armed monster. It didn't take that long for my senses to be trained to perceive such things as well. The other day I saw a nun walking across the snow. And I laughed because I saw a penguin in Antarctica in it.

And we had a blast. Omnec loved the music of the four pianists as much as I did, and we sang and jumped around on our chairs in the last row of seats, clapping and laughing and having a great time. Then that evening the last ice floes broke apart, starting only from me, never from her. Today we are friends, though she prefers to call me her "German daughter" because I am the same age as her only daughter Tobi, whom Omnec has just made a grandma. I travel around a lot with her, occasionally translating for her, and she stays with me from time to time.

With Omnec I always experience small miracles, which I have almost gotten used to by now. Often in the workshops and in personal conversations people start crying, experience a feeling of love that they have never experienced before, become like children again and overcome fears and doubts. What is also very noticeable is the fact that especially "outsiders" of society like drunks, homeless and however "crazy" people feel magically attracted to Omnec. Likewise children. They all intuitively know that they are loved and not rejected by Omnec and are always very happy when Omnec gives them attention and understanding.

Recently, in addition to the workshop on "The Transformation of the Earth", there is also a "Venus Love Workshop" where Omnec talks about what she is in my eyes ¬ love, unconditional love. She says, "The most important thing we need to learn here on Earth is to replace criticizing and judging with loving and accepting." Omnec teaches and lives love and unity, not fear and separation.

On one of our tours, we bought a bobblehead at a gas station. We were always happy to see one in the car in front of us. Omnec said "He is very positive." and imitated the head wobbling of the wobble, at which I laughed myself half to death again. That happens often, that we laugh heartily. Through them I learn to always and everywhere find something funny and to make something great and unique out of the smallest things and situations that seem difficult. Nothing can be so bad anymore that it can cause deepest despair and depression. There is always a light, a joy, a new way. Because every moment of life contains an experience that is precious.

"There is always a reason behind everything that happens. And if we don't see it right away, we will find one!"

Chapter 8 – Momentum

What goes up, must come down
What goes round, must come round
What's been lost, must be found.

– The Alan Parsons Project[4] (1978)

The momentum of breathing into the outside world has been going on for a long time. This is measured in linear time, because in higher-dimensional time nothing has happened, since there is always only now. Many know this thanks to Eckhart Tolle, because he speaks about nothing other than "the now".

> *The stream of thinking has enormous momentum that can easily drag you along with it. Every thought pretends that it matters so much.*

> *To stay present in everyday life, it helps to be deeply rooted within yourself; otherwise, the mind, which has incredible momentum, will drag you along like a wild river.*[5]

4 What Goes Up by The Alan Parsons Project, Pyramid, 1978 RCA Records, a division of Sony Music Entertainment, Composer, Lyricist, Executive Producer: Eric Woolfson

5 Quotes from Eckhart Tolle

I have set my intention to bring the momentum of exhaling into the outside world to a standstill and to turn it inward. In truth, I believe that this reversal has already happened, and that it is already occurring.

What is still running now is the momentum. There are still branches of thinking and feeling that still need to wind down. I believe that my writing and every breath that I take helps my consciousness to approach a major turning point.

By breathing into the outside world, I mean losing consciousness in thought. What Eckhart Tolle calls "momentum" is the thinking that one's thoughtstream brings. This is not unique to this incarnation, but is an accumulation of thought structures and belief patterns that have accumulated over many incarnations. In addition, there is also a general field or matrix which lies like a big thick cloud over the Earth to which all incarnated humans are attached, to which we anchor at the moment when we come out of our mother's womb. Imagine instead of just an umbilical cord, that each of us is also connected by a matrix cord.

Matrix cord means being conditioned to exhale, forgetting who we really are, and becoming part of a field that has everything in mind but the enlightenment of the individual, one's happiness, true love, abundance, self-realization and all the beautiful, amazing things which for many people still sound like a fairy tale or a Garden of Eden existing only in a fantasy world.

But that's not true.

The reversal of the momentum takes place, first of all, through the realization that what is going on in human existence is certainly not the whole truth of reality. So the search for more, for more truth, and for true love is where the journey to conversion begins.

Next comes the study and experience of the higher realities: the remembering. This means a conscious traveling on the road to knowledge. There may be moments of enlightenment, which for each individual can look different, can be stimulated by different triggers, can be of variable intensities, and can last for different lengths of time.

The spiritual world must get a request directly from you, before it may supply you with all the appropriate spiritual experiences that you seek. Ask and it will be opened and given to you. This is a spiritual law. Someone who has not walked the road of awakening may not be given an enlightenment experience, because it is simply not on their self-chosen plan in this current incarnation, and that is perfectly fine. You cannot force anyone to wake up, which is totally unnecessary, because every Soul has their own plan and way of experiencing itself, including turning away from the truth and the divine.

Through studying and experiencing higher realities, spiritual knowledge is applied and integrated into life. Inevitably, the point of consciously setting an intention comes, because one has recognized that the spiritual world delivers to one what one requests, and that one is the creator of one's reality and levels of experience. This implies a lot of personal responsibility. One must also learn to deal with everything that goes along with and precedes the delivery of what is desired, so that one's frequency is adjusted accordingly.

If, for example, I desire the fulfillment of the highest, divine love on all levels of being and set the intention to want to experience this, including the physical-sensual level, the perfect fulfillment with my true beloved, then I must prepare myself for this. I must first find, stabilize and express this high love within myself, and really, truly BE this high, divine love. I must give this love to myself in the way I desire my beloved to express it to me. Only when I love myself absolutely am I in resonance to be loved absolutely, precisely because my experiencing of love, my being in love, does not depend on what another person does or fails to do. This includes and even presupposes as a priority the absolute turning to the Divine, because the Divine IS true, unconditional, infinite love. Only if I AM THIS love, am stable, and have arrived in this LOVE from the Divine frequency, will everything that I AM enter into my field and be one with me.

On the high levels of consciousness, of course, it is already one and always has been, but to integrate and be this love also in the physical worlds, to be fully God-realized, is something else again.

But if, alternately, I lower the standard a bit and intend to realize something simpler, for example the reversal of another momentum, then the rule is still the same. First, I make conscious what I wish to end, for example, a marriage that has run dead and that I no longer wish to prolong. First, I make this decision inwardly, even before I tell my husband. I enter inwardly into communication with my spiritual team, and say: "I wish for a harmonious ending of this partnership. I ask for the right impulses at the right time, so that this intention is realized in the highest possible harmony with all involved and in unconditional love and gratitude." When I am finally quite clear and calm with this inner decision, and feel guided and strengthened by my spiritual team that now is really the right present moment, then I can communicate this to my husband in the highest way possible.

Of course, it is still possible that he sees it differently, yet it is also possible that he may agree and be relieved that I opened the dialogue. In the end, it doesn't matter, even if he makes a huge fuss and tries to put all the boulders in the world in my path to prevent this separation and keep me bound to him. Regardless of his reaction, I have the power of my Soul and of God's love behind me and within me to go forward calmly and relaxed.

Of course, that's easier said than done. However, that is the method: to become aware of what I want, to express it, to go into the experience, meet it, and ultimately to internalize it. That's how it goes, on and on.

Of course, as long as I remain in the momentum of exhalation and am in no way aware that I am the creator of my life, and then in a sense I remain a victim of circumstance rather than a master of my destiny.

The ball that is thrown upward comes down again. That is the law of gravity. Within those motions, there is a turning point, a moment of pause. It is the same with breathing: between each exhalation and inhalation there is a moment of stillness.

In this silence IS the creation.

Therefore, I must consciously seek out this silence in order to be aware of the creative power of my being and to consciously apply it. As long as I flow on the thoughtstream and am identified with it, I only act and react out of habit, out of programming, based on what is already there, based in a state of unconsciousness.

This is why what Eckhart Tolle has brought into our world is so important; namely, the constant, friendly reminder of the importance of silence, its significance and also its beauty. Because in silence creation takes place, and in silence there is absolute love, absolute freedom, absolute peace. In silence, the ego cannot survive. To step away from the eternal stream of adopted programming, thoughts, feelings, and old reaction patterns, the practice of silence is the way. Even a single breath without thoughts is a pearl.

I claim this because I know myself well and I know how incredibly difficult it is for me to go into silence and to dwell in it, to give priority to silence and to seek it out every day. Setting this intention alone has taken more than half a century for me in this life. Of course, I have often had experiences with silence, but so far in life, it has always been much easier for me to go into silence in the context of certain seminars than to seek it out on my own.

I remember, for example, the practice of Japanese ink painting that I practiced for a few years at the Felsentor in

Switzerland. There, through painting, the Zen meditation practice, and four days of silence, I had my first experience with silence, and wonderfully entered into tranquility.

However, back in everyday life, that tranquility was quickly gone, and I did not achieve it on my own, at least not permanently nor efficiently. I did not even manage to practice painting at home, even though I had purchased all of the materials including a small wooden table just for painting. But the matrix cord, which I still carried around with me and which had made up my typical everyday life, was always so dominant that I was never quite able to return to that wonderful stillness, silence and tranquility again.

Much later, in 2021, I explored "healer training" with Boris Lukacs in Switzerland, and under his guidance, the practice of silence is essential. In the energy of that group and through the great power of Archangel Raphael, who works hand-in-hand with Boris, the immersion in silence became possible for me again. Amazingly, my experience was better and more intense than ever before, because this I felt my direct connection to God, through prayers and powerful I AM affirmations. During this time, it was possible for me for the first time to genuinely integrate prayers and meditation very deeply and divinely into my everyday life.

No efforts are ever lost. All efforts have an effect, they leave their traces and at the proper divine timing, there may resurface memories, continuations and a profound deepening.

The divine realization is not in a hurry. It is patience personified, because it is always in the now. God is waiting for us – always and forever.

In chapter 16, I pass on to you some spiritual practices which have helped me and that I use myself. Further on, on the last pages of this book, I point to several links and recommended resources for whose existence I am very grateful, because they continue to be great teachers and sources of inspiration for me.

Chapter 9 –
Cyclic time – Linear time

We're so bounded by time, by its order.
But now I am not so sure I believe in
beginnings and endings.

– Dr. Louise Banks in the film ARRIVAL

Cyclic time, circular time, spherical time – the subject is complex, therefore I do not want to distinguish these terms here still. I call what I am talking about cyclic time.

The easiest way is to watch the movie ARRIVAL. The film is one of the most intelligent films I know.

Linear time is familiar to us. Past, present, future. We write from left to right, others write from right to left, others write from top to bottom. But in each case everything is linear – in one direction.

In our world and in our system a human being is born, recorded with name and birthday. His umbilical cord is cut, for this he is hung on the cord of the matrix. The first years he is still relatively free and may be as he wants to be, express himself freely and is usually also loved, no matter if he screams or laughs.

However, you know how being a human being works in our society and in our system.

If you don't fit in, you get in trouble and end up on the fringes. The highest good of the individual is not interested – it's about the collective, about believing in established systems and values – even in the calendar and time system.

Self-realization, truth, true love, and spirituality don't belong in our given system; instead, it's about fitting into and maintaining society. Everyone knows that money rules the world and that forces are at work behind the prevailing system that do not have the highest good of our Soul's salvation in mind. This is probably clear by now to anyone who reads a book like this. Manipulating and controlling forces have ruled the Earth and its societies for a long time. That is not an opinion, that is simply a fact. You can see this everywhere and all people who have kept a little freedom or find clarity in the course of life, see the effects of this subjugating prison system, which is also called matrix.

What is meant by "matrix," is simply a system of control, an artificially created matrix or template of life to which incarnating Souls dock and in which they usually function throughout their lives and to which they give up their life energy. The forces that control this matrix feed on the life energy of the Souls who believe in it and give it their energy. This has been permitted since many thousands of years ago in such a way because it serves the experience spectrum of all beings involved.

Now, with the coming end of a world cycle, this form of control over people will also end, at least for those who see through the game, set out to find the truth and create their own new world. This is what is meant by the separation of the two major timelines – one towards even more control, transhumanism and artificial intelligence – the other towards awakening, remembering Creator consciousness and returning to love.

In the linear time many old calendars come to an end, so I have heard, and therefore many people believed that the world would end or there would be an apocalypse. As I understand it, the control system of the matrix, that is, the identification with the consciousness of separateness, is ending because the Earth itself is going through a cycle completion and ascending to a higher frequency level. From my teacher Omnec Onec I got to know this topic as "The Transformation of the Earth."

A reminder: everything I write here is based on my own experiences, research and reflections and is permanently in motion. Words are two-dimensional. They can't depict a multidimensional reality. That's why it's always important to know that only your inner self alone can tell you what's relevant for you. Maybe something beyond the mere words resonates for you, which gives you a completely different inspiration and which superficially has nothing to do with what is written here. What I write down here is my point of view and not the ultimate truth.

I do not know on what sort of time scale from conventionally known time measurement the transformation of the Earth happens. I know however that it is an ongoing process and that it accelerates more and more. Omnec has always emphasized that how fast the process goes depends on people, and that all concrete prophecies are distractions because time is simply not linear and because we all create the future together, it is not fixed. On the one hand, the change in vibration proceeds gradually, that is, little by little, so that the embodied Souls can slowly adapt to the higher vibrations and, above all, also have time individually to tune in and find their way back into their conscious creative power. On the other hand, there can also be leaps, quantum leaps, that is. Suddenly everything is different, we are suddenly in a different energy, experience something like a spontaneous enlightenment and notice that we exist in a different energetic field. But this happens only after good inner preparation and not in a way that somehow endangers or hurts organisms or the Earth. Moreover, everything happens simultaneously and in parallel, and everyone experiences exactly that which resonates with their own frequency and state of consciousness.

There is an immense love and a powerful intelligence going on behind all this, and it has in mind the liberation of Souls and the awakening of people into their God-given, highest consciousness. This power has been in the background for thousands of years. It has always been there, because it has created all life and also guards it, and before this great plan it has also allowed the Souls on Earth to go through oblivion and they may even go through a time of control and manipulation.

However, this cycle is now ending. Whether you call it entering the Age of Aquarius, New Age, transformation of the Earth, splitting of the timelines – it is maybe all the same, maybe not. What I tell you here comes from my own feeling and from what I have experienced, especially from Omnec Onec, but also in the course of many years from other sources and everything always in coordination with my inner compass. I am not writing a doctoral thesis here and what I share here has no claim to perfection, absolute coherence or completeness.

I find it meaningful to be rudimentarily aware of the greatness of the universe, to recognize oneself and to create one's life in freedom in such a way as to live an awake, happy life and to be a conscious co-creator instead of remaining locked in a claw of control.

Many of us carry memories of high societies on Earth and other planets. We were born with them, and many of us wondered early on what could have brought us here. From the beginning we felt alien, unwanted, out of place and unfulfilled. I myself felt terribly homesick early on and didn't understand what I was doing here. I didn't find love, I didn't know what I wanted to do professionally, I just couldn't see my way through. But on the other hand, I was so well prepared and also docked into the system that I could at least function and survive until I was led into my first awakening by Omnec and little by little all the pieces of the puzzle began to fall into place.

Now I am sitting here in Turkey today and I realize more and more and more deeply that I have consciously come to Earth in order to remember completely, to activate the perfect love within me and to be a lighthouse that emits its light inwardly and outwardly.

Of course we have a transition phase and I too am still marginally connected to the system, I too still need to use money and the old time system, my body needs protection and a roof over my head. My awakening status varies, I sometimes feel more clear and centered and sometimes less. My nervous system has always been a weak point in me and I am still learning to be very mindful and loving with myself. Inner work or shadow work is now part of my daily hygiene. I am continuously observing and reflecting on myself. Meditation, silence and carefully sorting out what I allow into my field and what I don't, require constant remembering and conscious choosing. I am in the process of integrating the high energies while being mindful of my grounding and stability. We are not yet in the astral world or fifth dimension, but it is already much more present than in past centuries and millennia. The energy is steadily increasing and that means that the dimensions or levels of consciousness are becoming more present and depending on what we focus on, we can have much easier access to these higher, finer worlds than ever before.

New gates are continuously opening and subtle energies are flowing into the lower worlds up to the physical world or third dimension. And if we align ourselves with this, we have the higher forces much more easily available and can make use of them, we can learn to create consciously and to shape our world as we would like it to be and as it is also our birthright as free, beloved Souls. But the key is always love and acceptance in the now – because only in the present life takes place.

We need to stop reinforcing through our thoughts and emotions what already exists. What we see out there in the outside world, and the thoughts we think often and out of habit most of the time, are often not our own but are fed to us by the field we are docked to. These are of the past and keep us stuck in the matrix, OR they are the desired future of an artificial negative intelligence that wants to continue to control and manipulate us. Practicing discernment and truly going into our own heart is more important than ever and our ticket to freedom.

To escape the ruling system, we have to get out – and that does not mean to emigrate to another country or to burn our money overnight. The Venusians did indeed do this with the burning of money at a certain point of their development, but they were already further ahead than we are today, however, we are approaching this consciousness – there are only some intermediate steps to complete. The Venusians have shown it to us and if we listen to Omnec Onec and Dr. Raymond Keller, then we can learn optimally from them.

By getting out, I mean first and foremost getting out internally by stopping giving our energy to and believing in the existing system. Rebelling against the existing system or being against it in some way, that is, in resistance, is also strengthening for the system. This includes the belief in linear time, that is, the belief that this is the only thing that is real, because it is not. Time as we know it is a man-made construct that keeps us on a certain track and helps us function together in the third dimension. The matrix that has controlled and manipulated people for so long and the forces behind it make optimal use of the linear time structure to keep people in bondage, pressure them and suck their energies.

I'll give you an example to illustrate. For example, remember the times of the last century when working 12-14 hours was normal. I am taking an extreme example now, but imagine you are born into a family where the primary concern is survival. Imagine you are a girl. You are raised from an early age to be as well-adjusted and well-behaved as possible. You have to marry as early as possible, whether you love the man or not doesn't matter, the main thing is that you are a proper girl and soon have your own children and you can manage the household and the family. Your man goes to work from dawn till dusk and then he still has such his manly needs that you have to allow him to satisfy them on you. Maybe you like it once or twice, but at some point it wears off and it doesn't give you anything anymore, but you have to fulfill your marital duties – that's quite normal.

On the other hand, if you are born into such a system as a boy, then you have other burdens to bear. You have to show toughness early on, show emotions and crying is not possible at all, you have to find a well-respected and well-paid job or, if possible, take over your father's company, whether you feel like it or not, no one asks. You have to get married, whether you like the girl or not or whether you even like how she smells is not so important. You have to feed the family and at the same time you have to be faithful and be a good father to your children. The burden on you is very heavy and you look for more and more time off, meet with friends to drink or cheat. You don't really know anything like happiness and freedom.

Now think about how much time and space there is in such a constellation to turn to the truth, to really realize God – and of course I don't mean the God of a religion or church – in you, to be really happy, to find yourself, to find out at all who you are, what you love, what you are good at, to turn to real interests, not to mention other basic rights like learning and traveling, having fun and living in abundance. Normally – and many people in other countries and cultures still live this way or something similar today – your lifetime flies by, you suffer from certain aspects like unrequited love or other traumas, experience one or the other illness and various facets of drama, maybe have one or the other small joy, chase some illusions like the dream house, the big money, winning the lottery or the ideal wedding – yes, and that's it at some point.

And then you lie on your deathbed and exhale.

On your tombstone you will find your name and two years and in between a little line, and your whole life is contained in this little line – that's how Eckhart Tolle once put it so nicely.

That is linear life. Be born – run through life – die.

It's getting boring, don't you think?

In truth, life is so much bigger. There is so much more to discover, to live, to be. Yes, that's how it feels to me now as I write these lines – I have the feeling that this old, linear life just doesn't interest me anymore. I'm through with it. I want more, I want to be fully myself, to be fully connected to the stream of life, to experience more, to learn to control myself instead of being controlled by outside or programmed thoughts. I am only interested in the expansion into the higher realms. The linear may still be there and is a part of it, that is just in the transition phase. It still makes sense that we have a clock and a calendar and can orientate and arrange ourselves in this way – for now.

But it will be much more exciting when we learn again to communicate telepathically, when we experience synchronicities, when we pay attention to inner signs and messages, when we communicate with our spiritual team, when we consciously create our reality and come into control of thoughts and feelings and actions, when we explore the vastness of possibilities – and above all and permeated in everything – perceive the creative power, God, the Supreme Divinity again and are ONE with it.

When we experience LOVE again, feel our energy centers, meet our Soul families and twin flames and become one with them, when we celebrate real parties again, without drugs and alcohol, but draw from our body's own sources of happiness. When we learn to develop and apply higher technology, when we begin to travel through the universe and into other dimensions, when we experience all our senses and energy centers in the physical, because yes, I know, life even in the physical can be one big party – and that's why I think it's so important and worth striving for, that we turn to the higher more and more consciously, that we acknowledge the love within us and turn inward and find our Soul brothers and sisters more and more clearly and joyfully in order to create our world together with them – THE world that we really want to have and LIVE AS we really want to live.

In this sense: Let's roll up our sleeves ... (ooooh no ... just not like you might think now!).

But about "rolling up my sleeves," I just thought of something I have often thought about when I have been a guest in another country somewhere in the world – namely the garbage that is often still lying around everywhere. Personally, I love it when things are clean and tidy, and I've often thought that it's a sign of a backward civilization when it produces in a way that pollutes the planet. And that's not just production, but also people's consciousness. The careless throwing away of garbage alone, which is probably still practiced by millions of people around the world, reflects a certain consciousness.

I found it particularly conspicuous in India, there I have seen downright mountains of garbage in nature and at the edge of places. Also here in Turkey, even in the midst of the hotel castles in the few areas that are still undeveloped, there is still a lot of garbage and people still throw their cigarette butts around in the area.

What I associate with "rolling up our sleeves" is the idea that we could either be provided a higher technology by our more evolved friends or develop it ourselves to collect and dematerialize the trash on Earth with ease and joy on the land and in the seas. That would be so much fun! Imagine getting your hands on a great gadget with a group of Soul mates and going on a glorious hike with them, being able to dematerialize everything lying around like some kind of laser blaster! All cigarette butts, all plastic bottles, all stupid face masks, simply everything that lies around on the land and in the sea and swims around, could disappear so once and for all and by the extended consciousness and the new attentiveness of humans in their love for creation and nature nothing more would come to it. It would be still more amusing, if one would suck up its finds by its laser blaster and that one has then the energy to the order, in order to create in the end in the evening after done work together loud beautiful and funny things from the accumulated energy again and to take pleasure in them. Because, as we know, matter is energy and energy is matter – nothing is lost, everything can be transformed with the right technology. This is just one example of the application of wonderful, higher technology that definitely exists and is just waiting for us to discover it, receive it from the chronicles of the higher dimensions and harness it.

Now back to the distinction between cyclic time and linear time on the basis of the movie ARRIVAL. The story goes in short form like this: Alien spaceships land on Earth and give humans – represented by linguist Louise – the gift of cyclic language. Because Louise is called in by the military to mediate between the visitors and the humans, she is the one who learns to communicate most closely with the strange heptapods. During these conversations, a transfer of consciousness takes place, meaning that Louise is transmitted the ability to remember the future. For example, she sees the illness of her daughter, who is not even born yet. She also sees a very important piece of information that will change the fortunes of politics on Earth at a later date and prevent a war. The essential thing from the point of view of the extraterrestrial visitors is that they transmit the gift of perception of non-linear time to Louise so that she can pass it on to humans, because in 3000 years the extraterrestrials will need the help of mankind.

This is complex and conveyed very calmly and lovingly in the film, and despite the complexity it comes across well and understandably. The maker of this film must have received a deep inspiration and understanding of the functionality of cyclic time.

I think there are other films that focus on time and its non-linear ways, but I can't think of them right now. The movie Dejà-vu with Denzel Washington is more about Looking Glass technology, which is technology that allows you to look into past and future processes to influence them. In the movie Men in Black 3, there is a fifth dimensional being named Griffin who is a master of timelines and apparently has a total overview in all directions at any given moment – this is very cutely portrayed.

What does all this have to do with us now? I think I know that all of our existence is cyclical and non-linear and that we as Souls exist multi-dimensionally and also simultaneously in different linear times.

I find the concept of the Oversoul or the Overself particularly helpful in this context. In this concept, and I call it now consciously "concept", because I have not yet experienced or remembered it myself, but have only heard about it from others, especially from Lobsang Rampa and Dr. Raymond Keller, the Oversoul is the higher aspect of our consciousness, that is, the control center that directs all our lives, all our incarnations. In this concept, as a Soul, that is, as an aspect of my Oversoul, I may have lived, for example, at the time of Atlantis, at the time of Jesus Christ, in the Middle Ages, in the Wild West, as a native of Australia, as a tribal member in an African tribe, as a Cherokee Indian, at the time of the burning of witches and the Inquisition, during World War I, NOW, and in the possible future in a time of total technologization under complete control of a surveillance state à la 1984 OR in a time of the return of paradise with realized wonderful technology used by fully awakened conscious beings traveling through space and living as conscious creator beings in harmony with the love and Laws of the Supreme Deity.

Which future do you choose?

Chapter 10 – The Venus-Germany Connection

The Venusian village where I was born and raised is called Teutonia, which means "descended from Germany".

Omnec Onec, "From Venus I Came"

As I already indicated in the chapter about Omnec Onec, there is obviously a special connection between Venus and Earth and in particular also with the German-speaking area.

What I try to describe here is only the beginning of a hunch, because the overview of the whole subject has not yet revealed itself to me completely. I only give you some impulses here and if you are interested in more, you will find out more about it. Especially in the books of Omnec Onec and Dr. Raymond Keller all keys are contained altogether, but some things you really have to work out yourself if you want to recognize something. Not everything can be given just like that. Words bring impulses, but the truth is a realization that lies deeper than words.

One of the still existing difficulties in the complete revealing and grasping of the connections between Venus and the Earth and in particular with Germany is connected with terms like "race" and "guilt" and "sacrifice".

In this subject area it still needs much light and love, so that the truth can reveal itself. And I believe that also therefore I do not see everything yet, because it is not yet my task to have this knowledge let alone to pass it on.

But in view of the fact that it will come here one day to revelations, I share in this chapter my puzzle pieces with you which you can take up and put together later with further puzzle pieces.

Puzzle piece No. 1: Teutonia on Venus and the German scientist

Omnec Onec was born on the astral plane of Venus. Before she manifested her physical body there, she was prepared and trained by the spiritual masters of Venus. In the temple of history, she was shown that once a German scientist had visited Venus and that in his honor her hometown was named TEUTONIA because he had done a good service to the Venusians in a certain way.

I myself did not understand this for a long time. Since I had not yet any understanding of cyclic time and no idea of the possibility of time travel and the viewing of timelines, this statement of Omnec was beyond anything that seemed somehow conclusive to me.

On the other hand, I had and have the highest respect for Omnec's deep knowledge and know that she always has a good reason when she tells something specific. Nevertheless, I did not understand this story with the German scientist and her Venusian hometown Teutonia.

Much later, when I came into contact with the books of the Venusian historian Dr. Raymond Keller from the year 2021 and read that there was a man named Günther Specht in the Second World War whose rocket was diverted to Venus by the Venusians through a kind of wormhole so that the rocket could not do any damage on Earth, I became curious. Especially because Dr. Raymond Keller also mentioned the name Teutonia in his book, in this case a continent on Venus named after the German.

All of this is still mind-blowing to me, just as all of Dr. Raymond Keller's books really shake up one's brain.

But this way the thing makes sense and is imaginable – namely insofar as this German Günther Specht had landed in the past of Venus, when it was still physically populated, millions of years ago, and that he had helped the Venusians with something there with his technology, which he had with him. Supposedly, he was even brought back to Earth later, or so Ray writes in his second book in the Venus Rising series, titled "The Final Countdown: Rockets to Venus."

Image 10: Teutonia on the astral Venus.
Drawing from Ruth Platner, 1995.

Puzzle piece No. 2: Sister planet Venus

According to Omnec, Earth was colonized by different races a very long time ago. The red race came from Saturn, which are the indigenous peoples and Indians with their special connection to nature, the black race came from Jupiter, which are the Africans with their special talent for voice, music and rhythm, the yellow race came from Mars, which are the Orientals with their special talent for futuristic buildings and the white race, which were often described by UFO-contact persons as angelic beings, came from Venus. All these races, before settling in our solar system, came from galaxies far away.

The peculiarity of the Venusians in relation to Earth is the purely physical proximity and similarity of the two planets, which are also called sister or twin planets. Spiritually, as I learned from Omnec, the Venusians have remained a people always connected within themselves, without ever having been compromised by negative forces. I am sure that this is not unique to the Venusians, but the combination of the closeness between the Venus and the Earth and the peculiarity that the Venusians have retained pure closeness to the Creator Source explains their role in assisting the Earthlings and the Earth on the path of their evolution into a higher consciousness.

In simpler terms, the Venusians are closest to us and they carry the teachings of the Creator in pure form.

Puzzle piece No. 3: The Omnec-Anja Connection

Omnec came from Teutonia on Venus, Anja was born in Germany. Our Soul contracts and Soul closeness brought us together in this life. I experienced initiations and memories through Omnec's presence in my life and was trained through my life experiences to pass on the Venusian teachings myself. Although throughout my life I have not felt up to this task and have often felt overwhelmed, there has never been another person besides myself to take this role in my stead. It was and is as if this role was only for me and it was only a few years ago that I finally accepted it as my destiny. I know that I was born to embody and pass on the energy, love and teachings of the Venusians that Omnec represents through my own being. It is conceivable that my German nature as well as certain characteristics and abilities as well as my presence in the German-speaking field has a function in this context.

What is certain is that during my life I have learned all the essentials that I need to fulfill this role well. These seem to be little things, such as that I have brought a relative talent for the English language, that I have learned to write quickly through my professional training and am good with language anyway, that I can handle computer and internet technology to some extent, that I have brought the tendency to work, to be orderly and diligent and what do I know what else, which is simply useful in the overall package for specifically this service as a facilitator of the messages of the Venusians. In addition, my own Soul plan has left me the space to be able to devote myself completely to the training and tasks and not to enter into 3D bonds in fixed partnerships or to experience life with my own children.

Puzzle piece No. 4: Germany, land of poets and thinkers

From the German-speaking area a lot of spiritual things went out in the last centuries. By this I mean the fine arts, i.e. literature, music, art and also science and technology. I think it is possible that what is fed into the aetheric field of the Earth through the German spirit has a world-spanning reach and is very inspiring and influential on the overall events.

That which is still in the Earth field as threatening and guilty energy related to the Germanic field needs healing and the realization of the truth on all levels so that the full energy of the balance can be released. As long as this healing and energy release has not happened, the Venus force will still act partially veiled, but this does not diminish its purity.

Venus as a symbol stands for love, for harmony and also for the spiritual. Who thinks that love is meant here only in a romantic way, understands only a fraction. Here the higher love is meant, the divine love, the balance between the forces and the divine spirit, thus the highest intelligence, which is poured out through the prism of Venus.

Perhaps we can imagine the German-speaking world as a kind of prism through which the energy of Venus finds its multifaceted diffusion in pure form into the world. In this way the streams of love rain down as pure power of inspiration into the spirits of many people on Earth and bring seeds to blossom in their inner fields, from which the new Garden of Eden grows.

Puzzle piece No. 5: The Future of the Earth

In her lecture "The Unknown History of our Solar System and the Spiritual Transformation of the Earth from Venusian perspective"[6] Omnec has passed on a very large amount of information, which gives a far-reaching overview

---

6 The full transcript of this lecture is published in our book "Simply Wisdom and Love – Venusian Spirituality". See recommendations at the end of this book

into the past, into the background, into the present and into the future of the Earth.

According to their statements the transformation of the Earth takes place now, because it is the divine destiny of the planet Earth to be a paradise. This is how it was once created and this is how it shall be again in the future – a harmonious planet that gives a fulfilling home to a multitude of living beings. The Earth is supposed to be a symbol, like a kind of heavenly library, where all living beings coexist in balance. In order to come into its destiny and state as it was once created and meant to be, the controlling and manipulating forces must leave the Earth completely and permanently and this is the process of transformation that is currently taking place.

The influences and compromises are very deeply woven into the system of the Earth-people and the control by the long-standing power-holding structures is deep-seated. That is why the transformation of the Earth back to its paradisiacal state at a higher level than ever before is a long-term process.

The more people have this information and consciously participate in this transformation through their own expansion of consciousness, the faster the transformation is completed and people are free to experience a new era of their human experience.

Chapter 11 – Initiations

The fifth-dimensional party is happening in the present moment.

– Jen McCarty

It is obvious to me that life consists of much more than what we are usually taught and told from an early age. I particularly know this from my own experiences that I call, for lack of a better term, "initiations". I carry the memories of these life-changing transformations innate within me, and therefore they are frequency-wise present within my body-Soul-mind system.

By what I call initiations, I mean spiritual experiences that have fundamentally changed me and that have added new dimensions to my spectrums of experience as a human being. Before these experiences, I was not aware of these truths and depths of reality, at least not in this lifetime.

I believe that in cultures where and during times when initiations were still common and when their value still had meaning, they were usually associated with a ceremony or ritual. In my view, it is a clear sign of the de-spiritualization and flattening of societies that, for example, such important phases of life as growing up, i.e. the transition of a girl into womanhood and a boy into manhood, are not duly accompanied and initiated by appropriate initiation rituals. When did this just get lost and how did it come about? In the end, to put it simply, it must have something to do with the ever-increasing control by the negative forces that have been working for so long to strip people of their spirituality and natural, biological humanity, that is, to eradicate as completely as possible their memory of their true nature as Souls, as divine, beloved beings, and to do everything possible to ensure that they merely do not remember who they really are.

True initiation rituals are fundamentally important for entering new phases of life. The good thing is – they exist and occur *naturally*, even without people consciously having them in their cultures and thought systems. Initiations are divinely guided experiences that people experience when they arrive at a certain point in their lives. Initiations determine a beginning of something new and open up levels of experience in people's consciousness to which they have not had access before, but which have always lain dormant in them.

In modern times, therefore, people experience initiations without the permission of their society or its recognition, they just happen when the Soul is ready. Since they are divinely guided and happen in tune with the Soul's plan, initiations happen when the appropriate maturity to remember something is present and when the person is able to integrate newly ascending frequencies from within.

It is obvious that babies and very young children are purely and clearly connected with the divine universal love and truth, before they begin to identify with their name and learn other words and what their parents and so-called guardians model for them.

As soon as the connection with the language and the field of the adults begins, the truth fades away and is replaced with time by the matrix, thus by the artificial structure, by the mirror world or world of illusions. There are many terms for this and there are very good sources[7], through which you can get more detailed information about this. The essential thing that I am trying to describe here is that there is a way out of this matrix, out of this illusory world. At the moment, due to the increase of energies on Earth, we are receiving a much more intensive support from the light realms than ever before.

I have incarnated as a Soul in order to awaken to this knowledge and to fully remember who I really am. In order to receive these memories, I have experienced several initiations so far, three of which I am aware of in such a way that I can describe them along with their circumstances, symptoms and effects. I may have experienced other initiations that happened in other layers of my being that I am not fully aware of. By initiations I mean inner openings into the nature of reality, into the nature of my own reality and that of the greater whole; which is ultimately ALL ONE.

Since I was born normally on Earth and grew up in a field deeply immersed in oblivion and totally connected to the established structures, I had a controlled and manipulated personality just like most people on Earth, unless they were born to enlightened parents and were allowed to retain their true nature and memory of being a Soul through their parent's energy and consciousness and through the environment they grew up in.

Most people on Earth, like me, are born into the field of the matrix, indoctrinations and programs, and most are so deeply intertwined with it that they do not awaken to higher knowledge or remember reality throughout their lives.

This is completely value-free. Every Soul unfolds in its individual way; every single experience is valuable. Every

---

7 Sources to understand the Matrix include the Matrix movies with Keanu Reeves and the YouTube video by Robin Kaiser (German, captions on YouTube available) "The Structure of the Matrix" **https://youtu.be/I1zVyUxFTyk**.

Soul is an individual. It is for example an aspect of the controlling matrix that individuality and Soul consciousness shall be abolished. Mean people call this the "sleep sheep consciousness", that means the simple accepting and running behind what is already there, the perfect fitting into the existing system and sacrificing oneself and one's life energy to maintain it.

Souls who have incarnated for this particular purpose to forget who they really are and for the experience of separation consciousness while simultaneously being deeply identified with the matrix – the implemented programs and structures – usually remain in this consciousness for their whole life. However, many of them have contact at least at one point with an awake or awakening person. These are often the black sheep of the family or other people from the immediate environment, who are tolerated throughout life as strange, different, maladjusted and with alienation. Due to the overlapping of the energy fields, a transfer of consciousness nevertheless happens here in the unconscious, so that the Souls of those who had chosen the sleeping sheep stage for life are nevertheless born in their next incarnation with new aspects in their field, in order to come closer to these contents of consciousness and to further develop.

In the past millennia, there have always been individual teachers of light, individual Souls, who have attained enlightened consciousness during their lives and presumably maintained it. From my personal experience, enlightenment is an experience that is always present as a memory in consciousness, but that does not mean that the state of enlightenment must be present continuously in every individual case. There are no rules according to my experience and my estimation, I experience it in such a way that an enlightenment can also be a short impulse of light, which lasts longer or shorter and which is triggered by a certain event or encounter. This occurrence always brings its special consequences in the life of the person. But not every Soul awakens, is enlightened, and from that moment on sits permanently under a Bodhi tree and has flowers and food brought to them by pilgrims who hope to briefly get some light from the enlightened one and find salvation from the wheel of rebirth through his presence and by touching his aura or even his physical skin or through a glance from him, also called "Darshan".

I think something similar exists, but that is perhaps more for the Indian space of consciousness.

A person who has had one or more enlightenment experiences and then continues to live more or less normally has an environment and must also interact with it. So, in order to be a part of his world, an enlightened, awakened person also adapts his energy system to his environment. In Western cultures, for example, it is rare that a person who went through enlightenment experiences is being acknowledged by the people around him as a spiritual master or an awakened being. One consequence of an awakened person is, for example, that he has lost attachments to the matrix and the existing system and therefore often no longer functions so easily in the usual time-money-work structure. Consequently, he has to adapt his inner energy system in order not to end up in psychiatry, as a homeless person or otherwise totally on the fringes of society.

Yes, modern enlightenment is somewhat different from what we know from books and Indian culture. In other words, today the subject of enlightenment is modernized, and the modern enlightened person must continue to manage his everyday life and accomplish his consciousness work after his light experiences as well. This is not easy, on the contrary. Often I have thought that the "sheep" or "slaves" have easier lives, because they are docked to the system, live their lives in it, grumble and complain perhaps, have their enjoyments through purchases and sensual pleasures, get sick and go to the doctor or hospital, go on vacation now and then, but basically they function, get their money, build their houses, get married and divorced, buy bigger and bigger TVs and more and more powerful smartphones, and are integrated into a secure, stable social structure or cultural fabric until they eventually fall into a grave, much mourned or silent and lonely.

Those, on the other hand, who have incarnated to see through this system and grow beyond it by awakening into their full consciousness as divine beings, often feel blessed with wonderful experiences, but at the same time it is not easy for them to continue to function within the existing structures, to deal with money and bureaucracy, to get along with time and plans or company systems, to deal with the unawakened people around them and with everything that belongs to the three-dimensional, fixed Earth life in a relaxed and resistance-free way.

Yes, because being as relaxed and free of resistance as possible is quite important, because as an awakened or awakening person you know that resistance only creates counter-resistance and ensures that what exists remains, because it is nourished by your own energy of defense.

That is why the short, succinct wisdom of my dear teacher Omnec Onec is so essential over and over again:

> *The most important thing that people on Earth must learn is to replace judgment and criticism with love and acceptance.*

These words contain the essential keys that lead into the attainment of an enlightened state of consciousness: Love and acceptance. Other keys that I have grown to love and juggle daily on my path, I am going to share with you in a later chapter with the spiritual practices.

In-Drop No. 2: From now on there are six of me

Before I go back to the spiritual world and write further on the subject of initiations, I would like to write down a short interim report of my stay in Turkey.

From now on there are six of me.

That sounds crazy – like multiple personalities, right?

What made me think of it? Yesterday I read Jen McCarty's book "No More Crumbs", which is my vacation reading along with "Unveiled Mysteries" by Godfré Ray King. In it she describes the need for what she calls "parenting". Being a self-loving parent and to love oneself, that is, the inner child. That brings us to three. Persons number four and five the Divine Feminine energy of myself as Soul, as well as the Divine-Masculine energy of myself as Soul, which is also the "Beloved," my twin flame. And "person" number six is, of course, God or Mother-Father-God, my Creator, the Loving Presence of God, the Source Energy.

In my notebook I drew this idea as a hexagram, that is, two triangles pushed into each other. One triangle consists of God at the top, the Divine Feminine aspect of my Soul below, and next to it the Divine Masculine aspect of my Soul.

The other triangle has the inner child of God at the bottom and above it, on one side, the loving mother and next to it the loving father.

My inner family – that is how I am complete in my mind.

Just now I thought of this picture again after my sauna session and in the shower, because I feel very lonely here in this hotel in Turkey – on the outside. On the one hand, there are not many people here, which is very pleasant, because that makes it quiet. The few that are here are not on my wavelength. Most of the guests are couples and families who go to the sauna even with small children and always all dressed, which I just find strange and unusual. Also, of course, I see in it again a conditioning, a programming. Even the smallest ones are not naked. What problem do they have with nudity, I ask myself?

Earlier two older German ladies came into the sauna, saw me lying there naked, and one of them said: "Oh, one is allowed to be in here without clothes?" This immediately caught my attention and I said: "I'm not going into the sauna with my clothes on!" Then the other one said: "Yesterday someone from the staff said, one should rather wear something in the sauna, because of the other guests and the children." I thought I wasn't hearing right. Consequently, both well-behaved ladies wore independently of each other their bathing suits. I was therefore minimally outraged and felt slightly alienated, because these good ladies kept their bathing suits on only because of some other guests and their encrusted ideas of sauna sessions. And even in this situation, in which they were with me alone in the sauna, they did not allow themselves to relax and to take their bathing suits off as they normally do when at home in Germany.

Yesterday, there was another situation that showed me my aloneness. I was signed up for an a la carte fish dinner at the restaurant and the one overzealous and over-friendly waiter asked me if I wanted to sit with the one man who was also traveling alone. I looked to him and he seemed okay with it, but not too thrilled either, so I hesitated and then asked him directly, "Do you want me to sit at your table?" He nodded, so I sat down with what's-his-name. It was fine overall, but nothing more. He was an older man, dashing, with an earring, and well dressed, but those details aren't that important. No conversation really wanted to come up, so I practiced silence and being myself – I don't HAVE to talk if there's nothing to talk about.

Today is day number 7 of my two-week trip here, and once again I was alone all day.

While I was in the shower after these strange sauna sessions, a cute thought arose from within me: "From now on, I will only travel with my beloved!" Immediately, I corrected this thought and I felt modest, because how can I just claim that? I don't know it, of course, I have no control over my beloved and therefore I can't simply decide this. But what I can decide, and which I did, smiling inwardly and really promptly feeling better, was that "from now on there will be six of me", which means: I imagine that I AM my inner mother, my inner father, my inner child, my inner God-presence, my inner beloved and myself. This is a real beautiful family and we can have a lot of fun together!

And now we're going to dinner together, today fortunately again to the anonymous buffet, which is mega delicious and I do not have to talk to anyone. Bon appetite.

Illustration: My inner family

Image 11: Hexagram with inner family.
"From now on there are six of me". DF = Divine Feminine; DM = Divine Masculine, I AM = God-Presence.

My Initiations

There is so much that is obvious to an alert eye about the flattening, artificial technologization, and patriarchal and matrix-driven global social structure that has imprisoned incarnating Souls for thousands of years and sucked their energy and life essences – and one of those obviousness things is that spiritual initiations do not exist in mass consciousness and in the mainstream.

For a deeply in the system integrated, adapted person - if he can do anything at all with the term - initiations are something seemingly mystical, something that perhaps exists in India or that once existed among saints who have been assigned to some ecclesiastical system.

What I write here just flows out of me – please do not put it on the gold scale, but check for yourself what resonates for you and what is right for you. Everything else you can safely let flow through you. I am not writing here to stimulate discussion or to annoy anyone, I am writing primarily for those of you for whom there is something in the frequencies of my words and stories that reminds them of something in their Soul or stimulates them to embark on the path into their own spiritual upliftments.

The first time I came into contact with the concept of initiation was through the book by Elisabeth Haich (1897-1994) with the same title. I must have been still a teenager or in my early twenties when I read this book two or three times. I remember perceiving a very deep wisdom and truth in it. I don't remember the details of the book, I just remember that it was about astrology and initiation experiences in the Great Pyramid of Giza, among other things.

My Soul tells me that all this is true and that we used to have true access to such experiences, that there were real mystery schools, healing temples and that in cultures where there was at least one branch of wakefulness left, it was essential to preserve and pass on initiated knowledge.

That was all a long time ago, and at some point true initiate knowledge had to retreat inward because the time of the outer world and the enslavement and compromising of humanity came to the front.

Only in the course of the late 19th century, as far as I know, things slowly started to get going again and old knowledge was brought back to the outside world by new messengers, most of all certainly Helena Petrovna Blavatsky (1831–1891), who with her works "Isis Unveiled" and "The Secret Doctrine" and the foundation of the Theosophical Society made long-lost knowledge about spiritual masters and occult, i.e. hidden knowledge, available again.

Rudolf Steiner (1861–1925) also comes to my mind in this context. I admit that I have studied neither his nor HPB's works in detail, but I had almost all books once in my private possession or in my esoteric bookstore Lichtblick in Landshut between 1997 and 1999. I read a lot at that time, but I certainly did not reach the absolute depth of these wise books let alone understood everything.

Although I possessed and read an enormous number of books, for example by Alice Bailey, C.G. Jung and other luminaries of esotericism, psychology, astrology and spirituality, my spiritual search and research remained rather on the surface until my first initiation. Until then, I had not made a habit of spiritual practice yet. My first 27 years were years of preparation, mainly through my intellect and personal experiences, but they did not involve any spiritual discipline or structure – in other words, topics such as "meditation", "prayer", "inner work" or other practices that really lead into the depth of being were not yet present in my everyday life.

When I was 24, I did an astrology training in Berlin. That was something special, it was a training that went on daily for over a year. I assume something like that only existed in the biggest cities in Germany and maybe in the USA and in England. You might know that better than I do, if you also took these paths at the edge of society early on.

I also studied the Tarot, I dealt intensively with the symbolism of the Tarot cards. I understood that this is a path of initiation and that there is a lot of mystical knowledge in it.

Pure oracles or predictions of the future also made me a little curious, but I always knew that the Tarot and astrology are real wisdom systems, whose studies lead people into areas of knowledge that are not present in the normal, superficial society, in schools and in the mass media. On the contrary, if anything at all is reported there about astrology and occult knowledge or extraterrestrials and UFOs, it is often to make a mockery of these subject areas and, above all, to ridicule the people who seriously study them. If there were any documentaries at all, they were usually prepared in such a way that the broadcasters presented this information as entertainment and as long-gone historical knowledge. The viewer was usually informed in an opinion-forming way insofar as esoteric, mystical knowledge can be attributed to long-gone times of superstition and ancient cults – but we modern, enlightened people with great economy, advanced politics, technology, science and above all super-great pharmacy – we don't need this old silly stuff anymore, we are after all the future and not the past!

These are all programming of the matrix and most people on Earth are attached to it. In addition, a large percentage of all incarnated people still cling to established belief systems. How many millions still believe in the Catholic Church or Islam? Buddhism and Hinduism may seem to be more peaceful overall and less interested in doing missionary work and in wars with other peoples, but ultimately these are also belief systems that only in a few cases have led or are leading people into full awakening; although more often overall and especially in India, where there are masters and gurus in the sense of spiritual teachers and who are also recognized and respected there.

But I do not want to write a treatise here about areas in which I am not an expert, I am just chatting down here what my impressions and experiences are that I have made in the course of my life. All this is told against the background that

I have chosen a way of life before my incarnation which leads me into the awakening of my true nature as a Soul, as a beloved, divine being. Therefore, I have a more expanded perspective of the world and its systems than someone who is stuck with identification in these structures.

First Initiation – Omnec Onec

My first initiation happened through a glance, also called "Darshan", from Omnec Onec. It was not intentional; I believe a spiritual teacher or master does not intend such a thing. It is because of the inner realization that is present in a conscious being as energy and that is radiated through their aura, their frequency field and especially through their eyes. An awakened awareness is simply always present.

Her presence in my life was altogether Earth-shattering. Beginning with the first acquaintance over the anonymous television until the physical encounter in my bookstore as well as by her books, Omnec's existence was deeply impactful, revolutionary and fulfilling for me. It was a Soul's connection and a re-encountering, but at the time, I was around 30, I didn't quite get these terms yet. I mean, I understood in my head and in my heart that I felt a connection with Omnec, but the real depth and scope of it unfolded over the years and decades that followed.

In the beginning everything was enormously exciting for me, the woman from Venus as a new part of my life practically turned me inside out and I experienced sides of me that I didn't even know I had. By this I mean feelings of euphoria, extreme joy and enthusiasm, realizations of oneness, inner calling, also first experiences of divine guidance and synchronicities. Terms like 3D, 4D and 5D were completely foreign to me at that time, but looking back I know that through Omnec at my side I had first experiences of the fifth-dimensional realm of consciousness, which my little Anja ego and my mind could not sort in at all yet.

The impactful thing I experienced as my first initiation was an exchange of glances with Omnec during a workshop that she held in my bookstore.

It happened during her second visit with me, because the first time we met physically, I was a nervous wreck and still unable to feel her presence in a relaxed manner. It was all in all extremely exciting for me that a real woman from Venus – and not just any woman, but THE woman from Venus – came to my little bookstore.

For me Omnec was a star at that time, I could hardly believe that she came to a seemingly insignificant nest in Bavarian Germany, and then even a second time.

Only gradually my energy field and my mind got used to this fact and my enjoyment of this reality took on a more relaxed dimension.

Because only in the rest, in the relaxation, it was possible that my Soul could be reached by a calm glance from Omnec.

We sat with a small group of ten to twelve people in a circle of chairs in my bookstore when Omnec held her workshop. Wulf, the music producer she had traveled with, translated into German.

While Omnec was speaking, I slowly relaxed and at some point there was this moment of the "Darshan". Omnec looked into my eyes with her big, beautiful, green, loving eyes and through my eyes into my heart, into my Soul.

The essential of this energy exchange was my realization of unconditional love. I felt for the first time in my life what love was. Holistic love, divine love. It felt so round, so wide, so relaxed, so full of trust, so harmonious, so beautiful, at the same time also so grounded, happy, blissful, fulfilled, grateful. There is no single word for this and artists and poets create poetry, paintings, and music from such an experience. This is Venus. Venus not only teaches, she inspires.

Later, during our exchange of experiences and thoughts with the workshop group, I shared my perception. I told the group that I had felt love and that now I knew what love was.

I remember that Omnec listened to me attentively. She already understood German quite well at that time, but above all she always grasped with her open senses what someone was expressing by means of their energy. I can remember that my feedback touched Omnec very deeply. Perhaps this was one of the moments when she too knew that I would play a role in her life, at her side and for the mission of the Venusians on Earth.

It was not only easy to hang out with a woman from Venus, but also to find her super and to support her. Very few people understood that, let alone approved of it. At Omnec's side, one had to cope with all kinds of difficulties. It was not only the own consciousness expanding processes which were initiated and intensified by initiations, but one also had to deal with certain external factors due to conflicts with the ruling system and its representatives, who often came along in disguise of people close to oneself.

I wished everyone could view at least once into the world from the consciousness of an enlightened master. This way, they would be confronted with all they have unconsciously done to the most loving, wonderful, gentle beings. Negative thoughts and feelings can be very painful for an open, soft, warm-hearted being; they can confuse and hurt it, up to physical symptoms.

From my perspective this is one reason why we have had very few highly evolved beings among us on Earth and also why the Venusians and other extraterrestrials of similar kind keep away physically as far as possible, because the vibrations of strongly negative, totally manipulated people are difficult to endure for high beings and very contaminating.

For this reason, from the time of her arrival on Earth until about the year 2000, Omnec was regularly brought secretly to a spaceship to receive energy treatments and healing. Personally, I could never witness this and simply have to believe what Omnec said. She always said that this was only possible for her alone and that she was never allowed to take an Earthling with her. I have no idea how these meetings took place, because Omnec was always a lot around people and has no driving license.

At some point, these meetings were stopped. Omnec explained that she herself decided not to receive any more special treatments, but to live her life on Earth just as any other human being.

From that point on, she was indeed increasingly ill. She often needed to go to hospitals, and in 2009 she had a stroke. Now, as I am writing this book, we have the year 2023, and Omnec is living relatively well with the after-effects of the stroke. One doesn't know for sure and it may sound unusual, but perhaps it was the stroke that caused a necessary balance within Omnec's being that actually stabilized and prolonged her existence on Earth. God's ways are, after all, inscrutable. All that IS simply IS the way it IS, and there is a purpose and a reason behind everything. Immediately after the stroke, I remember it well, Omnec had the feeling that this severe impact on her physical self was the sign that her mission was completed and that she would retire now. After all, she had delivered everything, all her books had been published and there was lots of additional material and information available in CDs and videos on YouTube.

However, God and Omnec's spiritual guidance saw it differently and Omnec's stay in her body along with her mission simply moved to another phase after the stroke.

Over the following months, this first initiation uplifted my whole being into LOVE consciousness. Consequently,

I went through completely new life experiences. I felt detached, liberated and encouraged to experience and express myself in a before unknown way. I was unleashed. Omnec's love in my life gave me the green light, the free pass to really go for it and to just have fun. I gave myself permission to try things out, because I suddenly realized that I was unconditionally loved and free to do what I love to do. I didn't have that recognition before. Before, I was always on the brakes, I was afraid of clashing, I was afraid to be judged and criticized, I was afraid of people, I had no idea who I was and what I was supposed to be doing here. I was trying to muddle through life, but I was also always searching for love and truth, which Omnec initially brought into my life as an answer. All my life I was unhappy in love matters as well as unsuccessful with the usual things expected from a normal 3D-person in terms of business and financial matters. The areas I was really blessed with were my stable health and my sufficient intelligence and education. I was also blessed with a stable set of parents who always protected, supported and loved me in their own way, and I have always had at least one really good friend.

The initiation into higher love enabled me to have a new depth of experience. Connected with this first phase of awakening was an unhappy love story – a classic example of "looking for love in all the wrong places." I had picked out a musician and fell in love with him. At that time, of course, I could not see that he was only a representative of my divine beloved in minimal version and above all a giant projection screen for me. I absolutely wanted to have that man in my life as my husband; I felt it must be him – and I believed in this illusion for about four years. In reality, my object of attention was not interested in me at all, at most he found me a bit likeable and felt flattered by my chasing him; and with his social streak he was not coarsely enough inclined to reject me in a way that would have given me true clarity.

For years I felt encouraged to stay on him, to project all my desires onto him, to have my experiences, the eternally repetitive experiences of being rejected, of unrequited love, of begging for handouts, and of settling for crumbs. Pathetic and sad, yes, but how else could I have experienced it but exactly this same way? It was such a valuable experience, just as absolutely all experiences were and are valuable. I can tell it so easily today, because I went and suffered through it, and because this attachment bond has been cut since my upliftment to a higher realm of divine love and self-love. Thanks to Omnec's initiation into true love and thanks to the permission of this man's Soul at that time to make him the object of my desires for years, I was able to take giant steps into my liberation and self-knowledge.

At that time, I was working intensively with Sanaya Roman's book " Living with Joy: Keys to Personal Power and Spiritual Transformation". Through my first big steps of inner work and the permission I had given myself to experience and get to know myself, I gradually discovered what a huge projection I had thrown onto that man. In other words, I realized that everything I saw in him and why I thought he was great and why I wanted to be together with him, I carried within myself! To figure that out, I did all sorts of things – for example, I organized a piano into my apartment and got two piano teachers, one for improvisation and one for playing with notes. I needed to pull back the projection that the man I thought I loved so much was the greatest musician ever and that I need to have him in my life daily. I believed his music was so amazing and that if I was together with him, I could listen to his great music every day and that I would love to carry his guitar after him for his concerts. I healed this illusion by opening myself up completely, like a child, to playing the piano myself. My adult self was well aware that I would not become a pianist anymore by the time I was 30, but that was not the point. It was absolutely about the energy of projection – I had to physically experience and to prove to myself that everything I hoped to bring into my life through this man I didn't need because I had it within me.

An additional effect of the first initiation into divine love was that I became like a child again. Suddenly I was totally playful, happy with simple things and joyful. For me, just playing the piano that had miraculously landed in my apartment was a great joy. In addition, I enjoyed the piano lessons and practicing to play. At that time I was already a huge fan of Tori Amos, whom I consider one of the greatest artists of all time. I loved to at least look at her music books with notes, because of course I couldn't play her songs, but sometimes one of my piano teachers played some of her songs for me and I was feeling so happy with having live music from Tori Amos in my apartment.

While I was going through this phase of liberation and raising my frequency, I intuitively knew that this cycle of existence would be closed soon and that in a few months I would leave behind my projections as well as the whole city in order to start a new phase of life.

Second Initiation – Phaistos Disc

During this time, and I already told this in the earlier chapter about the Phaistos Disc in more detail, I started to work in the company Telelogic in the spring of the year 2000. During my daily copying activities there, I became aware of the poster with the discus and I experienced what I call my second initiation. That was the opening of my third eye by the beam of light that aligned from the center of the discus poster with the center of my forehead. Through my frequency preparations the months before, my energy system was already so expanded that I physically perceived this experience like a tingling and opening of my third eye.

It was quite special to experience within my own body what I only had read in books about chakras before. Suddenly I felt the opening of the third eye and the activation of higher senses, clairvoyance, heightened intuition, and total trust in spiritual guidance. All this in combination with great joy, bliss, and the feeling of abundance and richness.

Connected with this was the increase of vibration in my body, which I experienced as physical swinging. I also remember that I had much heat within me. At times I had the feeling that energy was spurting out of my fingers and my toes and as if I could see in the dark.

Over the coming weeks and months, this second initiation led to a further expansion and increase of my energy to the perception of being a three-meter-tall androgynous being of light, as I described in an earlier chapter. This was followed by Atlantis memories and my first visit to Crete, where, as I walked across the central square of Phaistos for the first time, I felt I had arrived home.

That was in September of the year 2000. My mind was scattered throughout the universe and I was simply a BEING in unity. I was aware that I no longer had an ego. At the same time, I knew that I was alone with this state of consciousness in my environment, because all the people around me were not on the same frequency.

Little by little the gentle descent of my energy began, since I was unable to permanently stay in this state of consciousness at that time. After my summit in Phaistos, the experience of the other side of the Phaistos Disc at the side of the Lord of Darkness followed, which swung the pendulum of consciousness experiences to the outermost edge of the opposite side.

Third Initiation – Twin Flame

My third initiation followed 22 years later.

I had neither expected nor consciously desired anything like this – I was okay with and content to integrate the experiences of the first two initiations for the rest of my life and to make the best of my life's journey. I already felt so blessed by life to have had such uplifting, wonderful experiences in the first place, and to have survived the dark so well. In the meantime, I was quite stable within myself, I had lost a lot of weight and on the whole I was able to cope with everything that belonged to this life on Earth in the third dimension. The experiences of the higher levels of consciousness, which I had made in connection with my first two initiations, were within me as memories and certainly therefore also in my energy field as radiation, but I was not anchored in the fifth-dimensional consciousness yet.

When the experience that I call my third initiation took place, there were still challenging issues in my life that I had to deal with, but I did not expect such a new spiritual impact, bathing me again in light and love and forcing me to find my lane in this inner roller coaster – how could I? Something like this is orchestrated by a higher instance; and the deeper recognition of this higher instance is one element that my third initiation brought with it.

Since this experience was just a few months ago at the time of writing these words, I am far from being able to reveal all the connections and realizations. I also cannot see yet what effects this awakening will permanently have.

However, I feel that I want to reveal the basic theme, which is the spiritual truth of Twin Flames. I dedicate the final chapter of this book to this wonderful information, describing some of what I have so far recognized and what I am able to pass on from my perspective at this time.

The mere fact that I am now writing this book and seeing it as telling the story of my cyclical existence is related to this new experience. I believe that further cycles are closing; my life has entered a new dimension of depth and the fact that I am now, for the first time in my life, not only writing my own first book but also seriously intending to publish it, seems to me to be one of the effects of this initiation. Why and for what exactly, I cannot yet overlook. My Soul has the reins in hand and knows what it does. My Anja ego is only the executing instance.

As for the symptoms of my third initiation, I can say that it has been a level of heart chakra center activation that I have not experienced in this way probably for thousands of years or since the descent of my consciousness into the lower worlds – at least not in embodiment. That which I experienced through Omnec's Darshan in 1998 was my first experience of divine unconditional love, but that which I experienced through the encounter with my divine beloved in 2022 activated an immeasurable dimension of love within me, a holistic Soul recognition and a realization of the Divine Feminine and Divine Masculine. Shortly after this encounter, I wrote in my diary, "I am drowned in love."

For me this is all very big, and I know that without my spiritual previous experiences I would possibly not be able to cope with the experience and integration of this dimension of love without getting completely off track. I am not, of course, the only one on Earth at present who has encountered their twin flame in embodiment. The twin flame incarnations and encounters are taking place more and more right now to bring the high, unconditional love through our own bodies to Earth and also to break down the encrusted, established partnership and relationship structures of the matrix and to download new, fifth-dimensional templates for the life of divine love in embodiment.

There is much more connected with this subject: It is about connections of hearts and Souls, about anchoring the Christ-Mary-Magdalene love, about initiation knowledge, about the return of the harmonious balance between the masculine and the feminine, about the healing of all wounds, above all the primordial wound of the separation from the Divine, about the realization of the Divine in the human being experience, it is about LOVE, about the stabilization of the Light, about the strengthening of the light grid, which is just wrapping itself around the matrix, penetrating it and through the increase of frequency ultimately breaking it.

I cannot see the time scales in which all this is happening. I know there are always time indications, prophecies and visions of all kinds, but of course this is 3D or linear thinking. What my third initiation has caused in me is the stabilization of myself in fifth dimensional consciousness with an intensity and clarity that I did not have before. That is probably why this initiation had to happen, because I was not allowed to rest in what I experienced before, because that was by far not everything. Learning never ends. Furthermore, in reality I was not totally stable and happy yet, so therefore another dimension of love and light wanted to arise within me.

The knowledge that is currently spreading globally is immense and the initiations are increasing rapidly. All the Souls that are embodied to carry and participate in the transformation process of the Earth are gradually waking up through different codes and activations and stabilizing their frequencies in higher consciousness.

Since you are reading this, you are definitely one of them, one of us.

Topics such as 3D-4D-5D and higher dimensions, timelines, transhumanism, artificial intelligence and the like are now the talk of the spiritual community, as well as the presence of extraterrestrials and their messages.

Now the Twin Flames are coming along as well, which is a very high level of love. In the further course of this book, I will share with you a little of what I have come to realize since my experience in this regard – and this process is still going on as I write these lines.

I want to clearly emphasize here that a twin flame encounter is a road of awakening and, of course, not the only one – albeit an extremely intense one. As I have made clear in this chapter, I have had other initiations before that were not directly related to my divine beloved. The divine beloved is within me, by the way, because he is my own Soul, or an aspect of my Soul. Words simply are not designed to adequately describe higher dimensional truths. This is really a highly spiritual subject and I know that I would not have been able to cope with it earlier in life – neither energetically nor cognitively. Had I personally met my twin flame earlier, I would have been mercilessly overwhelmed with this experience. Therefore, talking about "would haves" is totally nonsensical, because my spiritual guidance is in charge of all experiences perfectly – everything runs in the divine time schedule – the perfection of the universe is immeasurable. All that is simply so amazing! Absolutely everything is happening at the absolutely perfect divine time and in the perfect divine way.

This, by the way, is ONE consequence of my twin flame experience: I have never before felt so humbly and lovingly compelled to surrender absolutely and one hundred percent to God and, above all, also to acknowledge God as the only reality, because only Mother-Father-God – only myself as Soul, the God Presence within - has absolute knowledge and the complete overview. To minimally preface it – I clearly experience it in such a way that I remain arrested in human suffering if I do not completely surrender to the Divine, and that is absolutely uncompromising. In a twin flame experience, nothing makes sense without God anymore; everything that is now still ego and separation consciousness will inevitably maintain great pain or repeats it in loops until everything untrue is purged and purified.

Everything that is now still ego-personality must and will gradually become more and more surrender to the Divine, the livestream or the Universal, however you want to call the All-That-Is, and ultimately it will completely dissolve in the Soul and the divine guidance, because Soul and God are the only instances of truth and love, only in this consciousness love is pure, eternal and omnipresent. The ego is temporary, it is a tool to have its limited, restricted experiences in the third dimensional reality, and there comes a time when it becomes superfluous, like crutches, after the broken bone is completely healed.

Whether this total letting go of the ego crutch still takes place during embodiment, I don't know. I believe it doesn't matter. The essential is to observe it and to recognize oneself. I can well imagine it as Eckhart Tolle describes it: Using the thought process or the ego when it serves a purpose, but otherwise and predominantly be in the now.

The key is to distinguish pure consciousness from the ego. This can only be experienced in stillness, because only in stillness the ego is not present – and even if it is only a conscious breath that takes place in the now – it's an interruption of the stream of thought.

As soon as the thinking starts again, the ego is active and usually takes you somewhere, into the past or into the future. The ego doesn't want to have anything to do with the present at all costs, because that's where it disappears and that's what it naturally wants to avoid.

Only in the silence, in the zero-point zone, in pure consciousness – the ego cannot survive. In the now is pure being, or, as Jen McCarty so nicely puts it: The fifth-dimensional party is happening in the present moment.

Chapter 12 – Perspectives

Are you still wearing yourself out – or are you already "internalizing" yourself?

My Turkish orbits are "internalizing" me more and more. Today is day number 10 and I am looking forward to my return to Germany. But even more I am looking forward to the even deeper homecoming into my inner self, into my home.

I still have four whole days without a program. I was in a Hamam twice, once with the Dolmus in Manavgat up to the waterfall. I dyed my hair and had my feet pedicured. I walked around the hotel environment both on the streets and directly on the beach, and I also inquired about excursions, and up until now decided not to book one. So far I have not felt a clear "Yes!" for an excursion, which also has to do with the German-speaking Turkish men. I don't feel bothered as a woman, but I feel like I am a walking purse and attention tank.

I definitely feel that I have not yet completely returned to myself, that I am still preoccupied with the outside world, outside thoughts, outside feelings. I know the difference, I know how absolute love feels, how absolute panic feels, how absolute deep calmness and the feeling of being at home feels, and I still don't have conscious control over which state of consciousness I am in or how I consciously enter a certain state of being.

Of course, thoughts and feelings seem to be inside in contrast to the externally visible things, but in truth they are projections. I know the very deep silence, but I haven't succeeded in diving into it and staying in it longer – many mental activities catapult me out. I can imagine that nowadays I would succeed most easily in staying longer in the silence in a Zendo with zen meditations as well as in seminars with Boris Lukacs. Based on these experiences, I carry all spiritual tools within me. I know that I want to and will find my own way to connect totally to the Divine and to be in inner silence – independent of place, people, and circumstances. It is inner work, it takes effort and discipline to breathe in again and again, to internalize again and again, and to set a conscious reversal point after focusing oneself outwardly, to leave the train of thought and be in the zero-point zone in pure being.

Perhaps I will succeed in the next remaining days here in Turkey to go even deeper inside, but I'm not putting myself under pressure in this regard – I am already altogether so much calmer and more balanced than a year ago and especially after my third initiation, which has really triggered absolute inner hullabaloo. Possibly, in a linear way of thinking, I am even on the verge of arriving in my "internalization", in the deep silence, because on the outside I can't think of anything at all that I still want to do. This is exciting, because now I have four days ahead of me without a plan and that means I must and may again completely follow my inner impulses, let myself be led by my innermost, because my head is at a loss and only says: The plan is planless.

Today I fulfilled what seems to be the main reason for my trip to Turkey, because I went to the Hotel Daphne Garden, where I met Mustafa 33 years ago. Just a few days ago he told me via Facebook that he finds it exciting that I'm here now. He said that the house where we stayed back then doesn't exist anymore and that on this place today stands the Hotel Emerald. It's right behind the Daphne Garden, and I saw it from the outside today.

My walk to Hotel Daphne Garden was very interesting. I walked along the road between the hotel, where I am currently staying, along a shopping mile up to the shopping center in Side and a little further to the hotel. That was maybe six kilometers in total, for which I took my time leisurely.

I find it interesting that despite the overabundance of clothes and other stuff, absolutely nothing appeals to me here and I haven't bought anything yet. My observation is that there is total mass consumption here. Many unawakened men who are in absolute fascination with the smartphone world own all the stores. I don't use the word "unawakened" in a derogatory manner, but from my personal observation and experience, because they don't see eye-to-eye with someone like me. Either they just let me walk past them in peace, at least as long as I don't look at them, it sometimes works, or they chat me up like they are used to chatting up tourists. In doing so, they have no sense of how to deal with an alert woman so that she might feel invited to approach their store, browse in it, and maybe even try something on and maybe even buy it. I am so turned off by the way they sit like vultures in and in front of their stores and really seem to have nothing else on their minds but their cell phones and selling. It is impossible, without one of these salesmen trying to hook directly energetically deep into you, to stroll relaxed, to try, to ask for prices and above all to leave again without leaving a disappointed or offended person behind you, who finally shouts the very lowest price after you, just so that you might take something. So I really cannot go shopping and since I don't need anything urgently – I only would have bought something if the environment had allowed me to have a joyful shopping experience – I will probably fly back to Germany completely "unshopped". But we'll see – I still have four days, maybe a miracle will occur.

I don't like this oriental trading culture, maybe because I'm used to fixed prices and maybe because I'm still energetically uncomfortable with something that's behind it. Maybe there are countries or areas where trading would be a lot of fun for me. The people here are all friendly, without a doubt, but they feel trapped in these programs. I feel cordiality most likely with the regular staff, for example the waiters in the hotel and the massage therapists, and the dolmus drivers are fine too, because they have their prices and focus on driving and not on doing business. Since I know that the prices that the shopkeepers proclaim at first are completely inflated, I don't enjoy strolling around because I can't do it without getting involved in a conversation with the shopkeeper. In this exchange, I have to listen to all kinds of nonsense, most of which is not true and simply sales-orientated, and I am also constantly questioned about where I'm from and where I live and how long I'll be staying. Without going into this type of conversation, quiet shopping just doesn't seem possible here. That being said, I still quietly walked through various stores today and also strolled through the Side Shopping Mall – I didn't see anything I liked. The merchandise is the same everywhere and I couldn't spot anything which I found attractive. If it was hanging hidden somewhere, it didn't catch my eye because of the boundaries in the energetic field.

I see no individuality, no cute boutiques run by divinely awakened women, or at least by female women at all, even if not awakened. I have seen nothing but one-size-fits-all stores, one-size-fits-all hairdressers, one-size-fits-all tourist excursion offices, one-size-fits-all opticians, one-size-fits-all jewelers, one-size-fits-all supermarkets, one-size-fits-all bag stores. No bookstores at all, because no one here seems interested in reading. It's all the same and a hundred times over. All copied branded goods, all marked with some brand. That's the last thing that means anything to me, on the contrary, I don't wear clothes with brand names at all, because I'm not an advertising pillar or a billboard.

Likewise, when I arrived at this hotel, I did not accept to wear the obligatory wristband as a sign of my hotel affiliation. I carry it in my purse in case I have to show it to prove that I have my room here, but I don't wear it on my wrist. I am not a dog.

Another thing that strikes me is that there are no cozy cafés on the beach promenade or in the shopping area where I feel invited to have a Coke and a coffee, which I usually really like to do in between meals.

Today in particular, I felt a little like John in the 1988 film THEY LIVE, in which the main character gets a pair of glasses through which he sees the truth, namely the real messages on billboards and magazines such as "Obey!", "Consume!", "Sleep on!", "Get married and procreate!" and "Watch TV!". On banknotes he reads "This is your God!" and in a magazine are the words "Don't question authority!"

John also sees the real faces behind the apparent people who show themselves to him like mechanical skulls, and the more intensely they are interwoven with the ruling system, the more conspicuous is their behavior, which seeks to destroy everything that is awake and sees through the game.

In the end, it turns out that behind all this is an evil alien force that totally manipulates and controls people through TVs and money.

It's a bit creepy that such a movie carries so much truth, but not really creepy in the sense of scary, it's just eye-opening. A lot of movies carry a lot of truth and the Matrix series is definitely one of them, even if the complete story is not so easy to figure out[8].

When I arrived at Hotel Daphne Garden today, I would have liked to go inside and take a break for a drink, but I couldn't do that, because it was still closed. I observed that the work in hotel entrance booths is not reserved for men only. In this case, a Turkish woman was sitting in the hotel entrance booth next to the closed barrier and asked me what I was looking for. She told me that the hotel would not open until April 1 and that construction work was currently being carried out, so I could only look from the outside.

When I booked my trip to Turkey in Germany, the name of the hotel Daphne Garden did not come to mind. Only after my booking I thought of the fact that I could have traveled directly to Daphne Garden, because the completion of my Turkey-Mustafa-man-woman-cycle was after all the main reason for my trip – in addition to other reasons of taking a break from the German energetic field, sunbathing and enjoying the sound of the sea. But today also this detail was clarified when I learned that the hotel is still closed and therefore I could not have had a room there anyway.

I find this interesting because it shows once again that everything ultimately makes sense, even if you can't see it immediately. Often questions clarify themselves only much later and answers find themselves, which help to get an overview of connections. There are definitely always good reasons for everything, therefore it is always right and always wise to accept what is. Only the Soul, only the spiritual guidance has the overview, that is like the GPS, like the bird's

8 On YouTube there are videos with an Alexander Laurent (@EurasiaCouple) in which he explains in detail the symbolism of the Matrix series, among other things. "The second way of reading the Matrix trilogy" **https://youtu.be/d5BLE8vHRIY** (German, YouTube captions available).

eye view, but in truth it is even more, it is a holistic instance, which sees through all facets and life currents.

Another connection opened up to me when I sat down on the beach in front of the hotel and remembered how I used to spend time with my mother on the sunbeds under the umbrellas, which were absolutely vital in the summer sun, in August 1990. I remembered the mega-hot sand and super-warm sea and leaving my mother alone in the room in the evenings after maybe three or four days after we arrived because I was meeting up with Mustafa. I don't know if there were TVs with German channels in the hotels at that time and what my mother did alone. I remember very well that she didn't resist at all, she let me go and meet Mustafa. Maybe now, in retrospect, I'm even a bit surprised, but I know for sure that she didn't make me feel guilty.

Today, as I was lying in the sand in front of the closed hotel, resting a little after walking through the monotonous shopping miles of Side, I suddenly looked back from a Soul perspective at the encounter between Mustafa and myself and recognized another aspect that had not yet occurred to me. To validate that this is true, I would have to ask Mustafa, but it might well be that he cannot answer this himself yet. I feel that our meeting was arranged before our incarnations and that our coming together was not meant only for me to have my only beautiful experience with a man. Logically, there are also reasons for our meeting from his point of view, which I do not know completely, but from my limited perspective I have never thought about it, because I have always looked only from my perspective and that mostly from the view of the poor me, the woman who has no luck in love, the woman who is not loved enough by any man, the abandoned woman, the single woman with whom something seems to be wrong, otherwise she would have a partner.

Today for the first time the thought occurred to me that his Soul could also have chosen the connection with me, so that later in life he could come into contact with spiritual teachings, which he otherwise would perhaps not have found in this life. As a Soul he has chosen to come into the world as a Turk and to spend his life in the German-speaking countries. He had already gone to school in Germany and only later went back to Turkey, which is why he could speak German so well in the hotel at that time. The fact that he wanted to meet me was, in retrospect, nothing too personal. Our connection was not intended as a lived Soul partnership although it was a love encounter on a higher level. This is so important for me to acknowledge because the subject of LOVE is the most important of all for me and Mustafa's Soul has played a special role in my spectrum of experience in this context.

A common thread connects our Soul's plans. This is obvious by the fact that Mustafa contacted me again after 22 years in 2012. It came to a reunion followed by a renewed separation and resumption of the Facebook friendship 10 years later in 2022. I don't know if he knows anything about my spiritual activities. If not, of course it can still happen and that could be a good reason from a Soul point of view why we had this love episode in our young years in Side in this life in the first place. All pure speculation, I know – but it does me good, because it supports me in completing this cycle by looking at possible connections from a different perspective. With this cycle I no longer think that us two love birds are meant to be together in this lifetime. Instead, the healing of the wounded woman who has longed so much for a happy partnership all her life and has long believed that the fulfillment of life could be found in it. This might sound trivial, but I really don't see it quite so superficially since my first awakening experience through Omnec. The programs, indoctrinations and karmic layers were deeply seated and this is apparently really a decades-long path of transformation and healing of all unconscious, encrusted, frozen and misprogrammed levels of consciousness in this life.

This healing path goes on in phases, layer by layer. It's about more and more light, more and more heart opening, more and more truth – it's not just all done with a glimpse of light – it goes on and on, and the experiencing and the integration of consciousness goes on. Omnec has always said, "This is not the world of perfection; if we are perfect, we are no longer here." But love is the way, it is the only way back home.

For this life, I have decided to take the full portion of love, for the perfect realization and integration of the divine love and exactly for this reason I should not enter into a partnership at all. Because as long as I was not completely awakened, I would have also only come together with an equally unawakened man and we would have lived our common non-awakened life, as most people do. But all paths are different and my individual one was intended in such a way, chosen by myself as a Soul, that I dissolve bonds and do not enter into any new ones. I make out my consciousness processes alone, accompanied by friends, books and teachers, but not in the structure of firm relationships, marriages or even family foundations.

I am sure that in these explanations I can find the reason for the whole course of my life and as a result I can say that I am at peace with all that was. And this is the case at least until the time of my third initiation, because to meet one's own Soul in the embodiment of another person and thus to go into the healing phase of everything that is not yet completely in balance is once again another league. Another league of self-knowledge, of healing and also of suffering, because without going the way through purgatory and the dark night of the Soul, without once again feeling everything to the bone that constitutes separate consciousness and ego-identification, without really necessarily becoming aware of all projections and ultimately uncompromisingly turning inward and toward the inner presence of God, it goes no further to paradise – and that is ultimately the inner place of home where all cycles coincide, the nothingness where all timelines converge, heaven on Earth where God dwells in the heart and has his permanent place firmly and stably and at whose side I and my twin flame sit – in holy trinity, secure, loved, arrived. It is the true mystical path of enlightenment and ascension of the Divine within, and it feels simply immeasurably vast to experience everything that seemed to exist before only in books with every cell of one's being.

In this respect, the peace of acknowledging my single existence until the time of my third initiation was rather a kind of time-out, but not a real, deep peace, because otherwise my spiritual guidance would not have orchestrated this scenario. Before this new initiation I felt content with myself and my task to carry on the spiritual information of Omnec Onec and newly added by Dr. Raymond Keller and to go my way as a facilitator, ambassador or aspiring teacher of this content for the rest of my life – yes, in this I saw and see my deep calling and real fulfillment. I felt wonderfully guided, on the right path and at peace with continuing to walk this path alone.

The exciting thing is that this peace was abruptly lost after I had this special encounter and the connection with my divine beloved was re-established on the Soul level. Soaked in love and all of a sudden there was no more inner peace, because all at once all longings, unfulfilled desires, expectations, fears, doubts, non-stop thoughts, insecurities and deep hurts flowed through the layers of my consciousness and flooded my lower bodies, by this I mean specifically mental body and emotional body, which I define in combination as ego, and my physical body, for I had violent symptoms such as a burning, fast-beating heart, sleepless nights, being enormously agitated and hyper-energetic.

This area of experience cannot be described in a few sentences. Should you already have encountered your real twin flame, then you know many of the symptoms accompanied by such a connection in consciousness. In a few words I mean that obsessive thinking is connected with it, that is, you can't stop thinking about the person, it is the first thought in the morning and the last thought before sleeping. Especially in the first weeks thereafter, I also had a flooded urge to talk about it and understand what was happening – because right off the bat I didn't understand it all, and it started a fierce phase of desperate search for knowledge and understanding.

Furthermore, such an activation is associated with a restless emotional range, that is, I felt completely flooded with emotions, could hardly concentrate, fantasized a lot and dreamed in all directions. My range of perception was suddenly expanded, I had a much clearer intuition and inner knowledge of what is true and what is false. Physical symptoms were an energetically fully blossomed heart chakra, a giant heart that always beat very fast, an increased heart rate, associated with it energetic flows in the meridians, especially in connection with other twin flames. When I heard them or was in exchange with other twin flames, or when I heard something true, it tingled in my whole body and flowed. I also had an overactive mental body that tried to comprehend what was happening and, as a result, I consumed an extreme amount of information in order to understand what was going on and to deal with this new experience. It was the process of spiritual alchemy, which means I experienced the unfolding of areas of knowledge which transmuted into hands-on knowledge. I also went through extreme activity, the feeling of having to walk a lot in order to dissipate energy and also an irregular sleep pattern, usually sleeping 2-3 hours, then again hours of being awake. Sometimes spontaneous sleep for a few minutes and then again wide awake for hours.

Yes, really exhausting.

If you are one of those who believe that meeting your twin flame will bring the ultimate romance into your life like the beloved à la Richard Gere in Pretty Woman will propose to you with his Rolls Royce and a bouquet of roses and then you will sit for the rest of your life as a couple with God in the middle of it all in your Garden of Eden, while you enjoy the exchange of your kundalini serpents in all variations and the angels play the flute and harp and you sing along and express yourselves creatively in your individual way and just be in love and that's it; of course with God watching over you in fulfillment and you dwell in an eternal state of immeasurable bliss – well, then, thanks to my description, you may have gotten an idea of what a real twin flame experience can feel like.

I always find it so exciting and also really healing that in the relaxation, in the quiet and the distance from everyday life, I dive down into depths and gain insight into perspectives that help me get things round and complete cycles.

Often I thought to myself that it would be super to have a Looking Glass or at least to be able to visit and operate it in a Soul journey and to be able to see all the interconnections of the life currents into the past and future, all the connections of all Souls among each other, all the issues and challenges, all the reasons and explanations. Especially triggered by my third initiation I feel catapulted into a new expansion of dimensions and am confronted with the necessity of inner balancing, as I could not begin to imagine that this would happen to me in this intensity in this lifetime. I can't say it's the first time I've really had to grow, because the times around my first two initiations were definitely also very challenging – but what I've been experiencing now for a few months goes into a whole other level of experience with a need for healing and becoming aware of truth and love – and all this through the physical body and the integration of these high currents of light directly in the here and now. Before my twin flame initiation, I had not even had the thought of a Looking Glass because the realm of existence of such technology was not yet accessible to me – not consciously anyway. How can you wish for or see something you don't know about? Perhaps you have heard the story of Columbus and the Indians, also known as the "myth of the invisible ships"? This is about how the Native Americans supposedly could not see the incoming ships at first because they had never seen these types of objects before and therefore they were not present in their field of vision, in their space of consciousness.

I am sure that there is such a thing as Looking Glass technology and that looking at timelines is possible – both for the insights of individual Souls and their life plans and for the big picture – also interdimensionally, interplanetary and interstellar.

With which I make a transition directly into my next chapter, in which I come to speak about the topic with time lines and open further areas of knowledge, which have emerged in my conscious space in order to be recognized, integrated and also applied by me.

Chapter 13 – Cycles and Timelines

What is a Timeline?

A timeline is created based upon attention and intention.

Whatever it is that you believe will create a timeline, which is essentially a holographic reality in and of itself. There are an infinite number of timelines operating concurrently within the present moment of now and wherever it is that we choose to focus our attention and intention, is the timeline that we will empower and create in any given moment.

It is important to note that in any given moment, we are working with personal timelines and we are working with collective timelines.

– Jen McCarty, Twin Flames and the Event

In-Drop No. 3 – Intermediate Station Atlantis

Just now, as I sat on the beach and turned inward, a vision arose in me.

As I usually do, I concentrated on my inner heart point and imagined that in the center of my heart there was a star, just coming into visibility as in the evening sky, becoming brighter and brighter as the sky was getting darker. I imagined that the light from this star was illuminating my whole body and that my body was becoming crystalline, clear as a crystal.

In this imagination, my inner image suddenly expanded and the vision arose of being enveloped by a crystalline or transparent sphere and this sphere took me into the sea and deep into a city on the ocean floor, which I recognized as Atlantis.

I was taken directly to a temple I knew well and saw myself standing before the High Priestess and the High Priest, dressed in a beautiful, long, white and beige dress and open sandals. A few moments after me, my divine beloved appeared next to me – he too had just been brought to this place. He was wearing the same fabrics and colors as me, only in a male version. So there were four of us there – the priest couple slightly elevated with the great flame of the altar behind them and my beloved and I standing in front of them. He and I took each other's hands and heard the words of the High Priestess: "The journey seemed to have been long, but here in the eternal now-time no time has passed. You are on your way home now. The others are also on their way here. When we are complete, we will go back to our beloved star. You are blessed, loved and guided. The beacon inside of your hearts burns forever. There is nothing to do. You are one heart, one Soul – just as we are all a part of each other. We are now finding each other again. We are all one."

Cycles and Timelines

I am writing this chapter as a suggestion for you, so that you can educate yourself further in the subject areas that are of particular interest to you through books, seminars and videos by the relevant experts. I do not want to pretend to be well versed in all the topics addressed here – I am just sharing with you from my point of view what seems to be conclusive in my current state of knowledge.

I have been aware of topics like multidimensionality, timelines, technologization, twin flames, Holy Trinity, spiritual alchemy, synchronicities and matrix, just to name a few, to some extent for a long time. I read about these subjects, translated contents or had some kind of contact with one or the other topic through inner experiences even without being aware of the terminology.

I mention this, because these particular topics seemed to fly around my ears together with my Kundalini when my third initiation was approaching and especially afterwards and since then. Together with the opening of my heart chakra center in 2022, my inner being was opened up to a new dimension of love, and also to new dimensions of knowledge and connecting dots. Suddenly connections became clear to me, I was connecting with new people, I educated myself through many videos and had new experiences that brought more clarity and truth into my awareness. Intuitive perception and inner knowing of what is true and what is false became more intense. My ability to go within, to meditate and visualize reached a deeper level than ever before. It's as if I had spiritually gone back to school – and this goes on, although meanwhile a bit slower.

My perception expansion began at the beginning of the so-called Covid time in March 2020. From this time on I grasped more clearly than ever before what is occurring on Earth and how deeply the system programming is established. At first, I observed quite amazed how many people simply jumped on this mask and especially the vaccination bandwagon without thinking and questioning the narrative and media propaganda. For me, these were signs of fear programming and blind faith in mainstream, political, and pharmaceutical propaganda. I also developed a sudden allergy to mainstream broadcasts. Although I never watched much regular TV, and certainly not documentaries or news, after the Covid story began I couldn't stand that chatter at all anymore and basically turned off if I happened to have the radio on and the news started. I wondered more intensely than ever what motivated people to even put that kind of information in the media as speakers. When Covid started, I knew right away that if I had had a job, I would have lost it on the spot because I wouldn't have played along with the rules and the whole circus around it. I can say that with certainty, because I had similar tests of my authenticity before in life and in case of doubt and too much inner resistance, I always preferred the way out – I was never for sale or manipulable and I never found it reprehensible to make use of my right as a German citizen to accept state support. After all, I always knew that it was never my intention to receive governmental money and that I did not want to rest in this kind of support, but it has always been the better choice for me compared to a kind of self-torture by remaining in a work situation whose expiration date had been reached. I guess that's also why I didn't have to face this "truth-test" in spring 2020. Instead I felt allowed to use the time-out wonderfully for myself and my further self-discovery, for healing and my awakening path.

I found the pressure that the mass media and pharmaceuticals and political propaganda put on people, the rules and regulations, the coercion that was exerted not only from the very top, but above all from the people around, quite remarkable. For me personally, all this was a clear NO from the first moment on. NO, I'm not going along with that, no discussion, no way. The only thing I went along with, out of sheer laziness or inner refusal to get involved in the pressure exerted by the external rules and people, was putting on that stupid mask for a while so that I could at least go shopping and to the post office in peace. Everything else, without exception, I resigned for all these years. However, I never bought a stupid mask, I always took the ones that were provided somewhere and I used them multiple times. When I saw videos on Facebook with young women who put on fashion masks, who looked at themselves in the mirror and then chose the prettiest mask, that is, when a fashion was made with it, I noticed a new phase of the separation of the consciousness of people among themselves.

I have also never made a Covid test, let alone accepted a so-called vaccination. It crystallized over time more and more clearly what this is for a stuff that they want to inject and also preferably as a permanent subscription. No, that was and is for me all an indisputable no, I have accordingly not flown in an airplane for years – my flight here to Turkey in March 2023 was the first flight for three years.

It was and is obvious that thanks to my spiritual experiences, initiations and trainings in the decades before, I was free of fear and educated enough to be able to deal with all of this without letting myself be manipulated – on the contrary – for me the Covid time was a time of healing, awakening, reorientation and renewed realization of what is going on in our world systems, how deep the control and manipulation mechanisms are seated and not only that, but with what vehemence they push through their agenda.

Here we come to the topic of the time line split. Some speak of a kind of splitting off of a second Earth from the old Earth as in a kind of cell division, or of a new Earth, or of an Earth 2.0. Omnec calls this phase the *Transformation of the Earth*, she did not speak directly of a division, she spoke of an elevation of the vibrational frequency of the planet together with those inhabitants who can and want to go along, thus of the transformation of the human consciousness. Omnec also spoke about the removal of the negative forces from the Earth's system of influence and about the fact that the Souls who would not go along this path of awakening would be "recycled", that is, they would continue their cycles of reincarnation on Earth or elsewhere in the universe in new incarnations. Today, there is a lot of talk about the division of dimensions, especially 3D, 4D and 5D. From my point of view, these are frequency ranges which are differentiated from each other by the levels of consciousness and which merge seamlessly like rainbow colors.

I myself explain the time line split based on my current level of observation and knowledge, which is continuously developing, as that some Souls decide to stay in the 3D matrix with maximum control and manipulation including technologization, transhumanism, and other Souls decide to return home to the 5D unity consciousness and end their reincarnation cycles.

While some continue to give their maximum attention to the outside world, feed and strengthen it through their own Soul energy and continue to believe and trust what is imparted to them from the outside, others are no longer interested in being caught up in controlling systems where love, individuality, spirituality and freedom have no room. Whereby the latter includes the acceptance of the transitional phase, that is, of course we still have to act and function with the system, while at the same time we turn our focus inward and stabilize the rise of consciousness internally. In any event, it is my conscious choice to use the system while simultaneously stabilizing myself in a higher consciousness. An external exit is not my path at the moment, I am not planning on unhooking myself and to hitchhike with a backpack with no money and to see where the wind blows me. Personally, I need a stable place where I feel safe and where my technology works. With that comes all sorts of responsibilities like budgeting, bookkeeping, and juggling the system that still exists.

The two paths summarized differently: Some continue on the path of fear, of unconsciousness and acceptance of what is real to them, dwelling in identification with the ego and thus in separation from the Divine, whereas others walk the path of love, freedom, awareness and awakening to their true being as conscious creators and co-workers of God, creating their world self-empowered and aligned with the Divine.

3D is the world of separation, of extensive separation from divinity. 3D is the dimension in which we have been vibrating on Earth for thousands of years and in which we have exhaled, in which we have spent ourselves, in which we have forgotten our true essence as divine beings, in which we have entered into our karmic bonds that have led us again and again into the next incarnations in all possible variations. The phase in 3D was instructive and experience-intensive, also painful and sorrowful. Control and manipulation sat and sit deep and the Souls of the incarnated people were stuck for a long time – an awakening, a spiritual liberation and the exit from the wheel of rebirths was almost impossible, because the matrix was much too strong and tight, the energies too dense, the social structures too narrow. The incarnated Souls were trapped and their learning experience areas were mainly based on fear and not on love. True unconditional love was practically non-existent and the few true teachers who brought this love to Earth were either killed or deified or both, their words were misinterpreted and religious systems were established based on the falsification of what they symbolically lived and taught as pioneers.

Unconditional love on Earth has existed for a very long time practically only between humans and beloved animals, and between humans and newborns, perhaps into infancy. Among humans, the energetic influence on a newborn baby and its control based on the social system and culture he or she is born into already starts in the womb. Individuality and a right to happiness did not exist for a long time – but this is coming back to us with the transformation of the Earth. Awakened Souls bring higher frequencies of love and new templates for societies, families and love connections into the world.

The era of darkness and separation from the divine is now coming to an end. There is an illumination permeating the world and the Souls so that they have an amazing chance to step out of the wheel and finally evolve.

For this reason, the transformation of the Earth has been initiated, that is, the raising of the vibration of the planet. This goes hand in hand with everything else in our solar system, with the sun, with the incarnated and incarnating Souls who come as lightworkers and starseeds and those who potentially carry the higher, awakened consciousness within themselves and bring it to blossom in the course of their incarnation. There is also much help and guidance from benevolent extraterrestrials, I personally am most directly in touch with the Venusian Ambassador Omnec Onec and the Historian of the Venusians Dr. Raymond Keller. Inwardly and through my spiritual guidance I am also in contact with ascended masters, with all kinds of loving light beings who inspire, protect and accompany me and above all, more and more intensely with the loving God presence, the Source of Creation.

Many people ask themselves the question about the HOW. How does this transformation of the societies and the

Earth proceed, how can one imagine the split of the time lines? What is meant with the split of the time lines at all?

The essential ingredient for answering these questions lies in yourself. The intellectual understanding of something so great is not possible, because it is about overcoming the mind and reclaiming its energy to use it as a creative force – and this goes hand in hand with love and all-connectedness and not without it. As long as knowledge remains only on the conceptual level, it is useless for creating a new reality.

The exact processes lie in higher powers and are perfectly orchestrated and guided from the spiritual world of light. The essential thing is that you focus your attention inward and that you remember one hundred percent who you are – a loving Soul, a spark of creative power, an immortal, beloved being who is currently having a physical experience.

The thought process that we humans have been using here on Earth for thousands of years is manipulated and controlled and therefore always limited. Imagination and visualization are keys to creation, but in order to master these powers again, it is first necessary to reconquer the mental body and this goes through the inner path, through silence, through self-knowledge and through reconnection with the divine.

The complete transformation of the Earth is a big story that, in my opinion, a single head cannot grasp at all. We do not need a teacher who explains to us in detail how the transformation and the ascension of the Earth works. We need to simply be in the present moment, go into resonance with our inner teacher and our inner child full of trust, and let ourselves be guided from within. Everything we need to know will be revealed to us in divine timing. I feel it is my task to take care for my own balance and happiness, that I love myself beyond all measure, that I take care of my physical and material area of responsibility and that I know myself. By being aware of the loving presence of God consciousness within me, I naturally express it through my individuality as a beloved child of God and share my light and love with the world.

I am certain that the new Earth emerges this way; it thrives through the blossomed Souls who make LOVE, GOD, and TRUTH priorities in their lives. All those beautiful human beings who heal their fears and separation consciousness through love, who become like children again, who become aware of themselves, who reclaim their creative power and the power of the spoken word and visualization, who open their hearts and entrust themselves to the spiritual guidance through conscious aligning with inner peace and silence – these are the Souls who make an amazing new Earth happen.

Chapter 14 – Two Directions of Development

Some people continue on the path of fear, of unconsciousness and acceptance of what is real to them, dwelling in identification with the ego and thus in separation from the Divine, whereas others walk the path of love, freedom, awareness and awakening to their true being as conscious creators and co-workers of God, creating their world self-empowered and aligned with the Divine.

When I made a trip to the "Monkey Mountain" near Salem in Southern Germany with my friend Axel in the summer of 2022, where I had not been since my friend Claudi visited me in 2015, two things in particular struck me: First, they had abolished the acceptance of cash there at the time (whether this is permanent, I don't know) and only allowed visitors to pay with cards. Secondly, there were still some employees with Corona masks standing around, even outside, giving information to the visitors and making sure that one behaved as neatly as the monkeys.

The behavior of those people, who even outside vehemently wore and still wear masks, I have inwardly classified for me into the categories "brainwashed and maximally manipulated", "full of fear" and "belonging to a new belief system". I say consciously "the behavior of those people", because I do not know these people and maybe one or the other still changes his point of view. In exceptional cases it may even be that someone wears a mask for allergic reasons, but he would not be in his optimal environment especially on a Monkey Mountain in nature, where thousands of tourists are constantly running around.

What I'm getting at is that I see it as a sign of the one direction of development or timeline that is being consciously promoted by some seemingly normal people. By that I mean that such a place as the Monkey Mountain is certainly not totally controlled by the state and certainly no one there is being forced to stop accepting cash. The management there consist of people and someone or a group of cash abolitionists must have decided that they only want to accept cards.

The question is whether they are aware of the implications of such a corporate policy.

The more places decide to only accept supervised payment, the more this artificial timeline is strengthened. For this reason, at the moment I don't think I want to go to Monkey Mountain again, first of all I'm not such a monkey fan anyway, I just like other animals better, but most of all I don't want to support places that don't even allow me to visit there anonymously and with my cash anymore. Of course it's better if you know that in advance, and we still have the good internet to do a research. In fact, you might have to pay attention to such things in the future and, if in doubt, choose another place to go – or make a conscious decision to accept it and pay by credit card.

Have you already familiarized yourself a little with the information about the direction of the one timeline – that is, with the agenda, with the symptoms and all that stands behind the direction of development, which I now call here for the sake of simplicity the "Artificial Timeline" in contrast to the "Natural Timeline"?

Artificial Timeline (2D) and Natural Timeline (5D)

Many connections have become clearer to me in the course of the past year. My perspective is constantly expanding and changing, and I am continually learning. Please consider what I am sharing here just as a snapshot of Anja's current state of consciousness. It can all be quite different and above all it is certainly much more complex in reality. However, one truth is that everyone is individually responsible for what he focuses his attention on and how he creates his world. It is generally true that your feeling tells you what is coherent for you and what is not.

There is a video on YouTube by Robin Kaiser called "The Structure of the Matrix" which I have now listened to three times. The third time I took notes. I find it informative and well explained. It fits perfectly with all that I already knew and suspected, which was only not yet clear to me in this way of explanation.

Since I came into conscious contact with the concept of timelines and since I heard about the "Two Timelines" into which humanity is currently evolving – and I admit that I haven't studied the subject in total depth, but look at it from my inner perception and with my intuition and inner truth compass – I have understood it to be very important to become aware of what is happening on Earth, and this in a more intense and detailed way than ever before.

At the latest since Covid – and I can only say "Thank you, Covid time" – it is more obvious than ever for me through my own experience what is going on here on Earth and that the dark forces seem to pull out all the stops in the last uprising to keep as many Souls as possible trapped and bound. I knew all this since I received the information from Omnec about the transformation of the Earth, that is since 1999 approximately, but with the year 2020 and the Covid story the years of inner preparation paid off and I began to see and experience that everything that once was only theory is really happening.

Here I am giving you an overview in keywords of the way I distinguish the two directions of development or the two timelines for me:

Artificial Timeline (2D)

Transition from the 3rd Matrix (3D) to the 4th Matrix (2D). Matrix (2D) – Flattening – Digitalization – Technologization – Transhumanism – Manipulation – Forgetting – 2 strand DNA – Genetic Manipulation – Dehumanization – Desecration – Expenditure – 3D > 2D – Patriarchy or Matriarchy (male-female imbalance) – Linear Time – Matrix – Slavery and Control – Mass Consciousness – Social Fabric – Classes and Social Structures – Artificial Intelligence (AI/AI) – Negative Forces – Dark Forces – Agenda – Soul Light Stealing – Mental Body Kidnapping – Cash Abolition – Debiologization of the Human Organism – Prison – Walls – Fear – Distraction – Movement – Ego – Primordial Separation – Primordial Wound – Ego – Separation of the Hemispheres of the Brain

Natural Timeline (5D)

Transition from the 3rd Matrix (3D) to the 2. Matrix (5D) – Deepening – Enlightenment – Expanded Consciousness – Higher Dimensions – Remembrance – 12 Strand DNA – God–manhood – Ascension – Internalization – 3D > 5D – Divine Feminine (Divine Femininity) & Divine Masculine (Divine Masculinity) – Cyclic Time – God–Consciousness – Hieros Gamos – Unio Mystica – Mysticism – Initiations – Kundalini – Heart Chakra – Third Eye – Freedom – Love – Bliss – Joy – Creative Power – Self- and God-Realization – Home – Soul-Partnership – Twin Flames – Soul-Groups – Paradise – Technology and Spirituality as two sides of the same coin – Phaistos-Consciousness – Ascended Atlantis – Miracles – Synchronicities – Silence – Space Travel – Time Travel – Connection with Galactic Friends – Healing – Soul – Higher Senses and Abilities

Chart No. 1 – Two Directions of Development

I created the chart in this chapter after I got a deeper understanding about the different levels of existence or creator templates, which Robin Kaiser calls "matrix" or "matrices". Previously I had heard of the term matrix mainly in the context of the controlling and manipulating world à la Matrix film series and over the last few months, due to my own consciousness expansion process, it also became increasingly clear to me where my own programming is still stuck and where I may work on myself to reclaim love and freedom.

For me it is especially exciting that Robin Kaiser's explanations complement very well with the structure of the levels of consciousness as I know them from Omnec Onec. I have drawn a chart based on her teachings which I insert in chapter 17 as Chart No. 2 – The Godworlds.

The chart in this chapter shows that the divine plane can also be called a matrix, namely the primordial matrix or matrix number 1. This plane of existence contains all other designs. It corresponds to the divine unity consciousness or

– expressed in numbers – the dimensions 1 to 12. There is nothing real outside of God, to put it in simple words.

Robin Kaiser calls the 2nd matrix the mirror worlds. It contains the dimensions 1 to 6. In his video he speaks of the Luciferian life design, by which is meant it a counter design to the divine basic structure. The 2nd matrix is a mirror copy of the 1st matrix and offers a dual life experience spectrum.

In Chart No. 2 according to the teachings of Omnec Onec about the levels of consciousness it is shown similarly: There the God planes and the Soul plane represent unity consciousness and the underlying levels of consciousness are the worlds of duality. In between, Omnec taught, there is the etheric plane as a boundary between the worlds of unity and the worlds of duality. To the etheric plane one could perhaps also assign the function of a mirror, although according to Omnec there are also other qualities connected with the etheric plane, which I will return to in chapter 17 when I go into more detail about the Godworlds.

Robin Kaiser calls the 3rd matrix the satanic matrix. It contains the dimensions 1 to 3 and is contained within the 2nd matrix.

The special thing about our present time is that ALL levels of creation are accessible to us.

In the transition period, two development directions in particular are revealed:

1. Either the change to the higher level of the 2nd matrix, i.e. the existence in the 5th dimension (5D).

2. Or the remaining in the 3rd matrix within which just an even more narrowed and even more limited 4th matrix is built up, which corresponds to a two-dimensional existence.

> *"The fourth matrix is being installed right now. It's a digital matrix that works in a virtual world." (Robin Kaiser)*

In other words – each individual has the choice whether he or she decides for an existence in a world of digital codes or for the existence as a biological-organic being with analog life programs. With the entry into the 4th matrix the natural-organic biology is left.

In the 4th matrix the beings are very far cut off from the original matrix, from the divine consciousness. Here, feelings are abolished and the connection to the divine is no longer in the realm of experience.

Because this level of experience is so far away from the divine order, it has an even more limited lifespan than the 3rd dimensional level of experience.

The way of liberation from the 3rd matrix goes through awareness, through discernment, through gnosis.

The distinction between the 2nd and the 3rd matrix is essential to recognize what is based on which plan field and which space of experience is connected with it. (Robin Kaiser). In simpler words: Learn about the two timelines so that you can consciously choose in which direction you want to put your attention on.

Please note that everything can also be completely different, because nothing I write here represents an ultimate truth. Everything I write is my personal experience and thoughts and reflects what seems logical and reasonable to me at this time.

The rising energies in this phase of evolution are refining the energy systems of all people who have chosen to awaken, so intuitive compasses are also responding much more clearly to what feels coherent, neutral or wrong to you. The relevant thing is only how you react to something and in what way you resonate and what you do with the information individually. When it expands your consciousness, gives you a new perspective or even makes your heart resonate, I feel a stream of happiness coming back to me.

(next page) Illustration of the matrices and the two directions of development. Chart by Anja Schäfer inspired by Robin Kaiser's video "Der Aufbau der Matrix". You can download this chart in color from **venus-spirit.com**.

Two directions of development at the end of the 3D era

- The Transformation of the Earth -

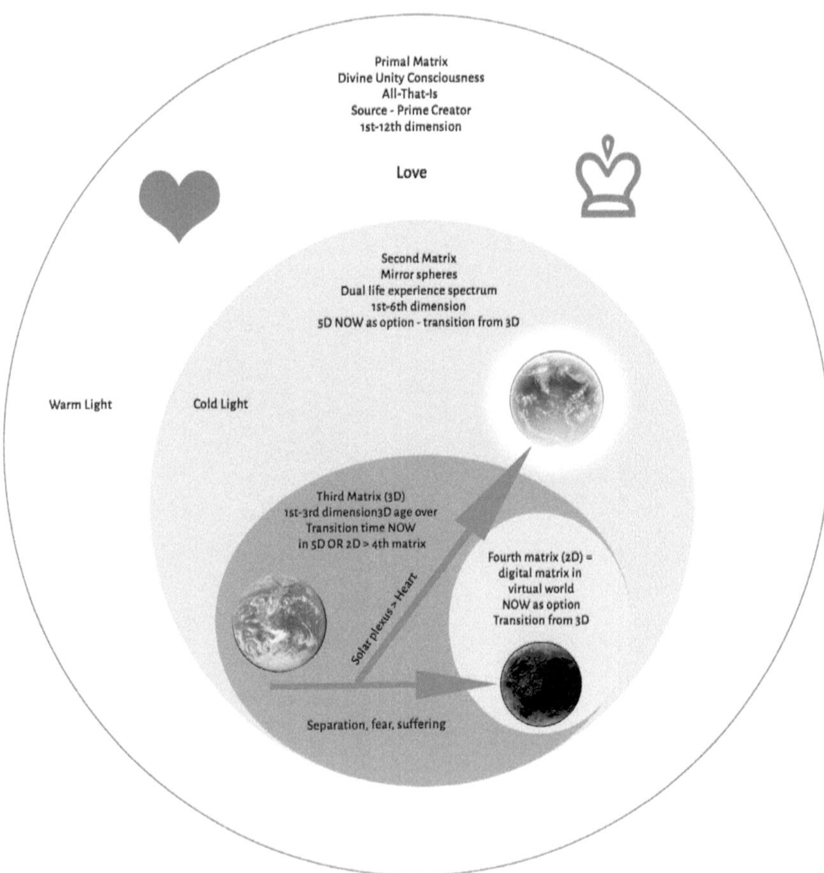

Chart by Anja Schäfer venus-spirit.com with reference to
Robin Kaiser's YouTube video „Der Aufbau der Matrix" (German)

Image 12: Chart "Two directions of development at the end of the 3D era"

Chapter 15 – The Transformation of the Earth

The Earth and humanity is now going through a transformation process – and everything will be as it was before the genetic manipulation. People will unite again and end all conflicts.

It starts with the fact that people's perceptions and views change. That is also the reason why I am here and informing about it. I teach people to overcome the structured and controlled perceptions.

When you are born here, you are given your religions, your political views and everything. Everything is taught to you from an early age – nothing is your free will, your free choice.

Omnec Onec interview with Jo Conrad, 1999[9]

The text from Omnec Onec, which I include in this chapter, contains all the essentials that she has shared about the Transformation of the Earth that is currently taking place. There is also a more detailed version published in our book *Simply Wisdom and Love – Venusian Spirituality.*

9 see Appendix for transcript of the complete interview.

The especially fascinating thing about Omnec's story is what she has to say about the origins of the Earth and humanity, and humanity's development, including genetic manipulation. This development is ongoing, including humanity's current transformation into a higher vibrational frequency. At the beginning of my years of training as a facilitator for Venusian spirituality, at the beginning of my cooperation with Omnec, I only heard this great information from her. Later, I translated Omnec's lectures and workshops, allowing the knowledge to penetrate deeper into my system and into my native language, so that I could better survey and integrate it with my mind as well. Still later, I transcribed and published Omnec's teachings. In parallel with this, my own experiences took place and validated for me in my own body and consciousness all that had in the beginning only existed in my mind as theory.

There is a feeling of enormity the first time one hears such great information. Then when one experiences its truth in one's own body, you have "walked your talk", so to speak.

I already felt ascension symptoms during my first two initiation phases around the year 2000, such as heart opening, a Kundalini experience, an opened third eye, the perception of my "Mickey Mouse ears", i.e. the chakras on the left and right above my head, and above all the memory of myself as an ethereal, androgynous light being with a perceived height of approximately three meters. However, all this disappeared again inside me. It was not that I forgot it – there always remained in me the longing for the recollection and return to this heavenly state of consciousness – but I did not *feel* this consciousness again for more than twenty years. That's how long it took me to integrate it and that's also how long I was spiritually not very receptive – I was oversaturated, so to speak, and had to digest it all.

Linear existence – cyclical existence – yes, it was more than twenty years in linear time until I returned to the next phase of remembering myself. In cyclical time it is somewhat simultaneous. In cyclical time the phases were just on different levels, a deeper or higher level. The spiritual journey somewhat resembles a spiral, and I've come back to the same point 22 years later so that I remember again and the journey inward goes even deeper.

Obviously, after more than two decades, my light experiences were integrated enough that I could handle the next serving of light without risk of my nerves burning out or me losing my mind again.

When I am alone, when I become aware of this perfection of divine guidance, I am lost in wonder and awe at the infinite love that permeates God's plan. The love for all Souls is immeasurably great and the increase in vibration takes place with absolute gentleness, so that the incarnated Souls are given time to integrate their experiences, to process them and, above all, so that they can decide which path they want to take.

I have realized that no Soul is lost – even those who decide now out of unconsciousness for the way into the deeper control matrix will be able to make a new choice at a later time. At least that is my guess. I don't know exactly what will happen to them. Perhaps some will also lose themselves so deeply in the depths of Artificial Intelligence (AI) that they will dissolve into it and be completely absorbed into the artificial structure of transhumanism. But in the end, everything is energy and is only transforming – in truth, there is nothing outside of the divine design of life because this is all that exists. Even the deepest control and the scariest appearing path of Artificial Intelligence are only aspects of creation, and therefore limited in time because of their remoteness from the Origin.

In the end, I do not need to concern myself further with the question of the direction of development of Artificial Intelligence, because I myself do not go this way and therefore do not need to give it any further attention. For me it is enough to become aware of the differences between the developmental levels. Then I look anyway only in the direction of light, love and God consciousness.

It is as if I arrive at a road junction and I look in both directions. One direction feels cold and dark, limited and lonely. The other direction is full of light, warmth, joy and loving people. Well, which way do I go? It's clear where I'm going; I don't even need to hesitate. I can perhaps pause for a moment and become really aware of this now-point, let my gaze wander in all directions around me, also look back to where I came from. I can also look up into the sky and feel the sensations within my body to see if I would like to fully perceive this now-point. It is, after all, a special junction in the road and many people pass by it and decide to go one way or the other.

Maybe I might have a picnic and watch the hustle and bustle for a while, that's super exciting!

Maybe I might also set up a small stand as an information office or tourist information bureau to help pilgrims understand their options. Maybe here will also be a gathering place for all my Soul friends, and perhaps from here will be where we board our Venus ship together when the time is right.

Ultimately, of course, I will go my way in the warm, bright, joyful direction with my Soul friends, for sure.

After this introduction, I share with you Omnec Onec's words about the history and transformation of the Earth. Omnec received this information in the 1990s, and has been sharing it in lectures from that time on. Her words form a kind of story, and this text explains the origins of the current state of the Earth and what each individual can do to bring about positive change.

In-Drop No. 4 – The Transformation of the Earth from Venusian Perspective

The Unknown History of Our Solar System and the Spiritual Transformation of Earth from a Venusian Perspective – Text by Omnec Onec (written in the year 1999).

In 1994, I had a meeting in meditation. I found myself in a valley, surrounded by thousands of people, human and non-human, among them people that I recognized like Paul Twitchell and Uncle Odin, of course. This is when they told me of the transformation process for the first time.

Since the 1930ies they had been working on it, creating the energy here step by step. There had been many meetings about it and needed the cooperation of many beings. Some did not want to participate, some did, and some beings from other galaxies just did not care. But they were convinced that the Earth is such a special planet because of all the different life forms that are on it.

So many different aliens had visited and contributed to the life here.

In order to understand the transformation and what the process is, you have to understand the history of this solar system, the human beings and the unknown history of the Earth. This was the information that was shown to me by the Masters and beings at this meeting:

About 40 million years ago – this is not precise because time is of no consequence, only the events are important and time is a concept created by man – from four different galaxies there were sent four different races of humans to this solar system. They were informed by the Spiritual Hierarchy to travel here and colonize the older planets. They were far more advanced that you can imagine. Not only did they have the ability to travel to different galaxies but also into different dimensions and to the future or the past.

They had telepathic abilities and no need of spoken language unless necessary for communicating with less evolved beings. They communicated with all life forms, animal, plant and mineral. They also communicated with those on other dimensions, who previously lived in the physical, angels, ascended masters, etc.

Their technology was in complete harmony with the natural laws of creation. They had mastered the concepts of creativity with the energy of their thoughts. This comes with the responsibility to use it for positive and constructive reasons that are beneficial and harmonic or for selfish reasons, such as gaining power and wealth.

They had complete understanding of creation and the creator. They knew themselves to be Soul and eternal, not restricted to the physical body. Death to them did not exist. For them it was a transition from one existence to another. They chose their own life spans according to the experiences they wished to have or missions they wished to complete.

They came to this solar system to bring human life here and to be the protectors of all life on all planets. The yellow race colonized the planet you know as Mars, the red race the planet Saturn, the black race Jupiter and the white race Venus.

Earth was then only a comet flying around as it had not taken the form of a planet or settled into an orbit around the sun. When the Earth finally became a planet, it was beautiful with large bodies of water.

The four races went to far galaxies and brought many forms of animals, fish, birds, plants and minerals and created a unique paradise where all life forms lived in harmony.

Within other systems there were also humans and other non-human beings that were not as advanced as these four races. However, they had the technology for space travel but still retained a more aggressive and conquering level of consciousness. They had heard of this beautiful new planet. At this time, Earth had two moons to harmonize the weather conditions and control the tides of the large bodies of water.

The first beings to inhabit the planet were a dinoid and reptoid race from two different systems outside our solar system. They were intelligent and walked on two legs like humans and were war-like considering themselves to be superior to all other life forms. In the past, the four races of humans had conflicts with them before they outgrew such behavior. They arrived on Earth to rob it of its minerals and valuable gems. Soon they had created a terrible war. They were joined by re-enforcements from their home planets. One set up its base on one of the Earth's moons, the other on Earth. It was a terrible war with advanced nuclear and laser weapons like you see in your science fiction movies. It lasted very long. Most of the life forms lay in singed waste and the one moon was destroyed. No longer interested in Earth, they went back to their planets leaving their wounded behind, they had no use for them.

The four races sent a few forces to see if they could help the wounded dinoids and reptilians and to see what they could do to repair the Earth. They soon found that due to the nuclear radiation it was too dangerous on Earth before it was cleared. Even they had to remain isolated so as not to contaminate their own planets.

Due to the radiation, the survivors of the dinoids and reptoids mutated into the Dinosaurs and giant reptilians you know of in your history. The humans that were trapped there mutated into what you call Neanderthals.

The Earth remained a devastated ruin, covered by a huge dark nuclear cloud and what vegetation was left was being devoured by the giant beings, also humans and animals by some. It was this way for hundreds of years before a giant comet crashed into one of the oceans and created another huge cloud. This created such darkness that the radiating heat of the sun could not interact with Earth's gravitational field and an ice age was created. This destroyed the mutated life forms and gave the four races the chance to cleanse and heal the Earth with technology and their energy.

Once again, they brought various forms of life to the Earth, creating again a paradise, except for extreme weather conditions and extreme tidal activities.

During this time, they realized that their planets were going into a natural dormant stage that they would not be able to support physical life. So they decided to colonize the Earth with their own people. They were concerned about the one moon, because it was creating Earth quakes and tidal waves and storms and other difficulties for the structure of the Earth. They knew how to drink fluids to protect and balance themselves. These were the first colonies like Atlantis and Lemuria.

The rest of the people stayed on their planets to await their destiny. They knew that they would perish and die. They had made the decision only to bring the younger generation with some spiritual teachers and elders to the Earth. The planet was too small for all of them. But they had no fear of death.

They had once again created a paradise. They were instructed to build special temples here as doorways to the other dimensions. There they could do their meditations and communicate with the higher beings. Because of the aggressive beings, the temples were hidden for future times when they will be important.

They were informed to build two shields around the Earth out of ice particles to balance the influence of the one moon. They created a tropical climate for the Earth. There were no deserts at that time. They had special crystals for these doorways and they were able to lower their vibration to enter through these doorways. The news spread of the beautiful planet. So the dark forces came here again, they were human beings but not as advanced at that time. They had a different genetic structure. They were very powerful but wanted to use this power for manipulating and controlling.

The people that were left on the other planets were doing a meditation at their last moment and as a reward the Spiritual Hierarchy told them that their culture would exist in the other dimensions and that this would protect the beings here. It was wonderful for them and it would serve a purpose in the future.

Another race of humans from a close system came here and tried to negotiate to get information and technology, but they were informed that they could not have it for fear of misuse and break of the spiritual laws. They declared war on the colonies. The colonies did not fight back but sent most of their people into hiding to rebuild the colonies later. They destroyed everything so that it would not fall into the hands of the dark forces. Lemuria and Atlantis were destroyed by their inhabitants so that their knowledge and technology would not be misused by the dark forces. Some people hid in the center of the Earth, were they are still living.

In this process the crystal structures were damaged, and part of the people that were hiding on the surface of the Earth were informed that there would be a flood on the Earth, because the crystal structures were going to fall and melt and cause a huge flood. So they were to build huge ships and save as many life forms as they could. There were hundreds of arks, not just one like we are told in the bible. They waited for the flood to recede, as did the dark forces. They came here once again to capture these people because they had realized that they were genetically different. They tortured them to get as much information as they could about the hidden temples to keep it for themselves and their power.

As they knew that the people could rebuild the Earth as long as they had their communication with the other dimensions, they separated their brain in halves of all the beings they captured, so that they would no longer have the ability to communicate with the other dimensions or remember their past lives, technology, temples, or anything. The human beings were reprogrammed and set up as different races and colors and they gave them religions and set themselves up as gods to be worshipped. Wars developed and the controlling forces were the rich ones, having all the information and power. It got worse and worse and today it is not different. It is continuing on a more subtle level, and the human beings have no longer an awareness of this. Although deep inside they have a feeling that there is more and they do look to the heavens and believe that they came from somewhere else, because they feel their existence here is not correct. Of course it is their Soul that does remember this, but the programming here is so complete.

The transformation is that all of these beings that have reincarnated since then and developed as well as the Spiritual Hierarchy themselves want to correct this. The first thing they did was to introduce the spiritual information here on Earth. There was an influx of information coming, and the esoteric movement grew in the societies and became more and more popular and common. They also contacted the leaders of the countries, but the cooperation was refused as they were not going to give up their control. The spiritual beings knew that they must save the Earth from going into destruction again and they knew that with the technology developed there would be more genetic manipulation here.

Furthermore, the invention of the atomic bomb was the risk that the Earth could be totally destroyed. This would have vast effects, not only for this solar system, but for the whole galaxy, and it would damage innumerous beings.

The Galactic Brotherhood (a federation of innumerous spiritually high evolved beings from different dimensions) therefore decided to put an end to this control, manipulation, and misuse. For decades, they have been working to change the whole energy of this planet so that the established technologies eventually would cease to function, but new technologies will be introduced when the transformation is complete and when the frequency of the planet and its inhabitants has changed.

All of the Galactic Brotherhood, many races – human and non-human –, the Spiritual Hierarchy, Ascended Masters, non-physical beings like angels, and the nature spirits are cooperating. Lady Gaia is the special angel for the Earth itself.

The hidden temples have been reactivated, so that also energy flows in from the higher realms through them. Space ships were located around the Earth to send vibrations to change the frequency. These ships vibrate at such a rate that they cannot be seen by human eyes or detected by radar, and they are continually sending their special energy to the Earth. The nature spirits informed all of nature to change its frequency – the birds sound, the bees, the water, the wind – everything has an effect on our environment.

The increase of the frequency is a gradual process. Approximately since 1993, when the hidden temples had been reactivated, it is certain that the process will be successful. They did not know it before, but the effort was made on so many different levels and with the people here. The more participation the faster the transformation will take place. They made it a gradual transformation, because the too fast changes would have damaged the cellular structure.

You have an artificial support system which is a new chakra system. It synchronizes the two brain halves to function as one along with the new frequencies, to give them back the abilities of their ancestors, to have mental telepathy, intuition, remember past lives, and receive individual spiritual information.

Chakras are miniature doorways to the energy of each dimension – there is a chakra for each dimension in the body. Children born after 1993 already have the changes within their bodies. They are born with the genetic system and the new chakra system intact.

While getting the new chakra system, there can be some physical uncomfortable feelings, such as short sharp pains like someone is sticking a needle in your body, you have your vision blurring, you have high-pitched sounds in your ears, or you will have rapid heartbeats. You will have times when you feel a little panicky, you will feel dreadfully tired even if you have rested plenty. Sometimes you will wake up after only a few hours sleeping and you will feel very energetic. Appetite will fluctuate, you will have times when you are constantly hungry and times when you don't feel the need to eat at all. All these unusual occurrences are temporary. It is important to drink plenty of liquids, to flush certain toxins out of the body.

Your intuitive abilities are returning, and your ability to communicate through mental telepathy with one another.

We have to realize that everything is valuable. Even the negative forces served to help us to experience diverse qualities of ourselves or to experience these qualities and possibilities. But some people become attached to having the power and the control and to use the life energy for control over others. It has been the problem that the people cannot overcome their ego and their tendencies to use each other and they use this energy for their own general self and selfishness.

In the future, the Earth will serve a different purpose than it has served in the past. It was more or less a place where that people could encounter the opposite energy from the Soul – the yin and yang, the negative and the positive. Of course, in reality it is the same energy. The division has been created by concepts. By determining that this behavior is bad and a different attitude is good, you divide the energy into good and bad. This way, you also help support the negative process.

Our ancestors were totally selfless people. They did not want to destroy or damage anything that was from the creator, from nature, because they felt in harmony with it. It was a natural way of surviving with the existing life forms in this physical world corresponding, communicating, and cooperating with them. These are the things that are going to be reinstalled in the human being.

In the past, during the original colonies on Earth, the feminine qualities were ruling. The people were more using their intuition and the feminine principles of loving and caring. Then, after the genetic manipulation, the male energy was controlling the societies and individuals with more force, more destruction, more might. In the future, the Earth will serve as a place, where that the male and the female powers will be equal and balanced within every individual.

Furthermore, the Earth will serve as a purpose for human beings to experience everything in one life cycle. They could manifest a body of choice. It will not have to be male or female, it could be both energies and qualities in one, because the physical body will not be of the same material as it is now and it will be on a different frequency.

People will form communities and connections and will work together with the animals and the different life forms. The Earth will be a totally different place than you know.

With the collapse of the negative powers, the aggression will recede, and there will be no need to actually overpower others or to be in charge of something. Every person will be in charge of their own selves and of creating their existence. The fear will be removed, and we will not have the need of the manmade laws anymore, we will just naturally obey the spiritual laws, because as an advanced Soul with a full consciousness and awareness, you will be able to govern yourself in a way that is in harmony with everything that exists.

We have lived that way on other planets for millions of years. It is just a natural harmony of obeying the spiritual laws.

It takes a lot of willpower and acceptance to go through this process individually and accepting the changes that take place in our societies. You only have to help to visualize and to create these possibilities. Imagine what it can be like or what you like it to be like, and eventually you will have that. We can look forward to actually creating what we are, what we wish to be, what we wish to experience rather than being forced to experience what already exists.

I hope that this information can inspire you and gives you the courage and ability to face whatever will come and accept it as the divine will, because whatever happens in the continuum of life is always meant to be. You have to learn to accept things and depend on your creative abilities to see you through the difficult times. But you have assistance from the other beings who have an alternative method of power and energy for you to use.

In the very far future of the Earth, after the transformation is complete, it will be a totally different living style and a totally different awareness on the Earth.

The thing that I hope that you can remember is: A Soul is perfect, a Soul is beautiful, and individual and complete. You have to remember your own beauty and qualities, that every experience that you have ever had in your creation, in your life cycles, is a part of what makes up the special jewel that is each individual Soul. This beauty and these qualities are determined by your individual process and development through your life experiences. There is no end to your existence. You have eternity to look forward to, when you can overcome the concepts of time and aging. If you can be happy and really appreciate the preciousness of life and experiences, then you have a better chance for a beautiful life and enjoying. Of course, you should enjoy every sense that you have in the physical world, because these senses will not be the same in the future, as the physical body will be totally different. You have to enjoy the different aspects of being a human being, and of course creating a balance and a harmony within yourself, because you are the only one that can do that.

I hope this information is valuable and that you can share it with others, because the more people consciously and actively participate in the transformation process and start using their energy in a positive way, the faster it will go.

I would like to leave you with a Venusian greeting which means "May the Universal love and blessings be": AMUAL ABAKTU BARAKA BASHAD.

Chapter 16 – Spiritual Practices

I AM LOVE.

In this chapter I would like to share with you some exercises and thoughts that I have made a habit of practicing. From experience, I know that applying these and other practices keeps me in balance and aligned with God consciousness, or help me return to the zero-point-zone when I have lost conscious connection.

I hope they inspire you to apply them. Or maybe they inspire you to go in search of other impulses that feel better for you personally.

The spiritual path or the path of enlightenment is individual. This information is not conveyed and taught in schools, established religions, and societies. Or have you ever heard in the newspaper, in a mainstream TV station, at school or in the normal circle of acquaintances and work environment – just anywhere in the 3D world something about the serious engagement with practices that guide into the presence, God realization, and enlightenment?

I remember well that in the final phase of my teenage years and as a Soul that was already incarnated in this system for almost twenty years, I realized through career information centers and at school that what REALLY interested me did not exist in our societies, universities and education centers. What REALLY interested me were topics like spirituality, astrology, tarot, self-knowledge, Soul, mysticism, other dimensions and worlds, and enlightenment. Well, by now it should be clear to all of us why this is like that on this beautiful planet. The time has come that we give attention to finding truth and finally take the scepter of self-empowerment back into our hands where it belongs. Equally, every individual's crown belongs on one's own head as a symbol of recognition of themselves as a beloved, divine daughter or as a beloved, divine son of the infinitely loving source of creation.

It is the recognition of this divine presence that this chapter is about. Most of us have forgotten that they are infinitely loved, immortal Souls and how to remember this truth. Being born in the established, compromised system and being interwoven with the structures of the third-dimensional matrix for many years, most incarnated Souls have lost all their memories during the first years of embodiment. That's why texts and books from teachers, their lectures and committing to a spiritual practice is so immensely important. Also, connecting with other like-minded Souls is becoming more and more important in our times of transformation, so that we focus our combined lights on the visualization and creation of a new world in peace, freedom, and happiness.

Ultimately, only ONE practice is needed – that is BEING IN THE NOW.

I myself am due to my mental body, personality, or ego and perhaps also in regards to my Soul mission as a facilitator of Venusian spirituality not so easily knitted. I personally need to wash my brain in various ways, and I have been doing that for decades. Until today, my mind has been too complicated to just find and commit to ONE exercise. We are all individuals, I personally like to try out many things and to practice what feels best for me at certain periods of my life.

Obviously it's not supposed to be that I just jet off through a spontaneous enlightenment in a steady state. I make detours in my consciousness, I travel through cycles of awakening and going back to sleep a bit – I evolve myself in a spiral fashion, every now and then a giant download and then a phase of integration and balancing. In these phases I stabilize myself through all sorts of practices like specific thoughts, affirmations, prayers as well as reading and listening to texts.

In the following I give you a selection of the practices that I really use habitually. I hope that one or the other matches for you. Many are inspirations from other teachers and as far as I remember their names, I mention them with love and appreciation. In order not to add too much around it, I give here only the short form without further explanation – you feel yourself what resonates with you.

As a suggestion, I can say that these words most intensively work accompanied by deep, conscious, relaxed breathing and when you say them loud. Of course, they also work in silence and everywhere and at any time. The most important thing is to remember and apply them.

Usually, I stick some of my favorite affirmations on post-its on my bathroom mirror.

Autogenic Training à la Anja

I AM calm.
My body is sitting (lying, standing, walking) here pleasantly heavy and warm.
My breath is flowing calmly and regularly.
My heart is beating calmly and evenly.

My solar plexus is streaming warm.
In my Hara center I am one with Being.
In my root center I am stable, supplied, calm and safe.
My forehead is pleasantly cool and fresh.
My head is clear and free.
I AM calm.

Healing Prayer according to Boris Lukacs

God, you are the love within me.
You are the life force within me.
From you I receive guidance and balance.
I acknowledge you within me.
For you are my source and life.

God, I call upon your love.
Please heal me.
Please send me the angels of healing.
For comforting and blessing.
My body, my Soul and my spirit.

Rest as awareness for a short moment according to Jen McCarty

Rest as awareness for a short moment.

Just stop thinking for a moment.

Stop thinking.

Jump off the thought train.

Drop the story!

Yin and Yang thought stops according to Eckhart Tolle

I radically refuse to harbor thoughts.

I have no complaint whatsoever.

Morning thoughts according to Viviane Chauvet

There is no greater service than to be of the light. Every day, when I wake up, when I come back to my body, I take a deep breath, and I say, "What blessing hold this day, how can I be of service to the light?"

Heart Star Meditation according to Peter Mount Shasta

A star appears in my heart as in the dusky evening sky. I direct all my attention to this star. It becomes brighter and brighter and illuminates my whole body, which I imagine like crystal, like very clear rock crystal. In this light I sit. I perceive the voice of the star, which speaks: "I am light. I am love. I am God. I am you. I am that I am."

Head-in-Heart Drops according to Q

I command my spirit to take the thoughts out of my head and put them in my heart.
5-4-3-2-1
And so it is.

I command my spirit to take the thoughts from my head and drop them into my heart to bring me peace.
5-4-3-2-1
And so it is.

How-to-just-be-Program from Omnec Onec

I am in the present – the now.
All is perfect, whole and balanced.
I do not believe in old limitations and lacks.
I do not judge but accept and understand.
I am as I was created to be perfect and whole. Free of the past it has no control only to learn from it.
I open myself to the wisdom that is part of that which created me and is part of me and within me.
I move on to the new, forward to release old patterns.
The more resentment I release, the more I can receive and give love.
I love all as I wish to be loved.
I see myself as an individual – unique and special.
All my experiences have formed the facets of the special jewel like no other which is myself.
I see myself as soul and this body only as a vehicle for this world. For I am part of the Creator and the energy that I come from.
Every day I am what I choose and think thoughts that create what I choose.
I allow all to be what they choose.
I am balanced in all I do.
I am not a victim of circumstances or other's standards but the master of my destiny.
I am whole.
I achieve the greatness that I am.

The Laws of the Supreme Deity according to Omnec Onec[10]

There are seven basic laws and seven divine laws of the Supreme Deity.

The seven basic laws

1. Know ourselves to be part of the Creator.
2. Be thankful for the experience of existing.
3. Not judge but accept all beings.
4. To know we have existed as all living forms.
5. Fulfill our responsibilities in each life cycle.
6. Obey laws of nature and societies in which we exist.
7. Learn from mistakes so as not to repeat old lessons.

The seven divine laws

1. Love all living creations.
2. Use our energy to support our worlds.
3. Share knowledge and wisdom.
4. Understand the equality of all souls.
5. Never use power to manipulate or control.
6. Know that the soul is immortal.
7. Give thanks to the One Divine Being daily.

10 The How-to-just-be-Program and the Laws of the Supreme Deity are excerpts from Omnec Onec's "Handbook of Venusian Spirituality", DISCUS Publishing, ISBN 978-3-910804-11-1

Affirmations

This is a selection of my favorite affirmations. Feel free to use what resonates with you.

These affirmations are inspired by Jen McCarty, Viviane Chauvet, Abraham Hicks, teachers of the I AM presence such as Boris Lukacs, Peter Mount Shasta, and Saint Germain – and of course I come up with my own creation from time to time.

I am now aligned with the divine.

I have now arrived as the truly healed version of myself.

I am now plugged in to the God source within.

I am the object of attention of Source energy.

I AM LOVE, I AM LIGHT, I AM GOD, I AM YOU, I AM THAT I AM.

I AM guided by the light.

I choose to let go of all fears and all expectations now.

May higher truths be revealed to me now from the realms of illumination and enlightenment.

I choose to be the sacred embodiment of light.

Chapter 17 – The Godworlds

If you imagine a centrifuge and put stones, sand and water in it, you will observe that the densest material, the stones, accumulate on the outside, then comes the sand, then the water, and in the center is pure energy. This is how you can imagine the center of creation, which we call God.

I created the "Godworlds illustration" in 2010 for Omnec Onec's book "The Venusian Trilogy". For me it is often easier to come to a deeper understanding of something when I look at images and illustrations, so when a subject really interests me, I sometimes create something visual myself.

In this chart you see the structure of the levels of consciousness as Omnec Onec passed them on based on her Venusian teachings. Frankly speaking, these are universal teachings, and there is no copyright on the truth.

Perhaps you have heard of Eckankar. Eckankar is the name of a worldwide spiritual organization that is returning the same teachings as Omnec to the people. Since Eckankar is an organized group, I would like to add that Omnec and I were never members of this or any other organization.

The founder of Eckankar was Paul Twitchell. Paul and Omnec connected physically in the late sixties during a lecture that Paul held. It was a Soul's plan with the intention that Omnec would receive the inspiration and impetus to begin sharing her life story and to eventually go public. This meeting in the physical on Earth was planned by the masters and other incarnated Souls involved, like Omnec's ex-husband Stanley Schultz. So that Paul and Omnec would recognize each other on Earth, he had already seen the Venus child Omnec together with his master Rebazar Tarzs during a Soul journey to the astral plane of Venus. During this journey, he learned that he would recognize the little Venusian later on Earth and that the two had a mission together. Until Paul's sudden death in 1971, they actually worked together, and originally Omnec's autobiography was supposed to be published through Eckankar. Due to Paul's transition, however, things changed and her book was published later by Wendelle C. Stevens in 1991.

Image 13: Paul Twitchell and Omnec Onec.
1971: Omnec is pregnant with Zandar.

Image 14: Wendelle C. Stevens and Omnec Onec.
The retired US Air Force pilot, UFO investigator and researcher published Omnec's autobiography for the first time in the USA in 1991.

There is a chapter about the Godworlds in Paul Twitchell's "Spiritual Notebook". That information corresponds to what Omnec later passed on in her own books and workshops.

> *We came to the polar worlds as a Soul for one reason only: To gain experiences that lead us to become a conscious co-worker of the Supreme Deity – REAL LOVE. Real love is the energy that flows from the Creator and supports all forms of life. Without it, nothing can exist.*

Consequently, we are all universal beings and not limited to one existence. There are no limits to love.

– Omnec Onec

As follows I am giving a short description of the illustration:

Anami Lok, or the dimension of the divine, is the world of oneness, unity consciousness, the source of creation, or what we simply call God. Of course, this does not mean a church or religious God or Allah, but the source of all being, which is pure love. There is nothing real outside of this God plane – everything that exists is created from it.

The **Soul level** corresponds to the dimension in which Souls are created in groups and from where they make their journey through the levels of consciousness, that is, to the polar worlds or worlds of duality.

The **etheric plane** is the boundary between the unity and duality or mirror worlds. According to Omnec, it is also the plane of masters and angels and of the individual Soul's knowledge that it is an aspect of God. It is also the plane of initiations and realizations.

The **mental level** is the level of thinking and conscious creation through the power of imagination. On this level the manipulation of consciousness occurred, that is what the people on Earth have been experiencing since the fall into the polar worlds. The recapture of one's mental powers is therefore an essential element of the return to unity consciousness and awakening as a conscious Soul.

The **causal level** is the level of remembering. Here all the experiences of the Souls are stored and can be retrieved through the Akashic Records.

The **astral plane** is the plane of emotions and feelings. It corresponds to the dimension on Venus where Omnec lived before she manifested a physical body and was brought to Earth as a child. The astral plane can also be called the fifth-dimensional plane of consciousness into which the Earth and the people who have chosen this ascension of consciousness are currently evolving. In her autobiography, "From Venus I Came," Omnec describes how Venusians experienced a very similar evolutionary process as people on Earth are going through today and how they mastered their ascension.

The **physical plane** is the plane of physical-sensual experiences, the plane of organic-biological human beings and other life forms into which Souls can incarnate, such as minerals, plants, animals and also other beings which are not yet so evident to us again on Earth.

Only recently I realized through the information of Robin Kaiser in his video "The Structure of the Matrix" that there is still a more condensed dimension below the physical level and that this is currently under construction. He calls it the 4th matrix[11]. I describe it in my words in the way as I currently understand it. From this perspective, this denser level corresponds to a further separation from the divine by entering a digital world where artificial intelligence has control over consciousness. In this dimension, organic-biological life ends.

In the Godworlds illustration you can see drawings, colors, mantras, and sounds that, according to Omnec, correspond to these levels. Visualizing, chanting, and learning about these dimensions facilitates the awareness of the respective level. I can't say anything more about the rulers, because I have not dealt with them more deeply so far. I only know that SUGMAD is a name of the Divine and that SAT

11 see Chapter 14 – Two Directions of Development

NAM is the ruler of the Soul plane[12]. I have included the ruler names in this chart mainly for the sake of completeness. If you are interested in this topic, you can find more information by doing research.

In the nineties a very beautiful meditation CD was created in the music studio together with Omnec's music producer Wulf Wemmje. This meditation CD is made for you to take a Soul journey through the levels of consciousness, let go of your mind and learn more about yourself. You can learn more about this CD, which is also available as a download, in the back of this book under Recommendations.

12 There is a visualization exercise in Omnec's trilogy and in our book "Simply Wisdom and Love - Venusian Spirituality", which describes the opening of a well starting from the Soul level. It is said that starting from the Creator (SUGMAD) and carried out by the Ruler Sat Nam, a gate was opened into the lower worlds so that the Souls trapped in the polar worlds would be liberated and find their way back into unity.

Chart No. 2 – The Godworlds / Levels of Consciousness

Dimension	*Mantra*	*Sound*	*Color*
Anami Lok (God Plane)	HU	Music of the universe *(cannot be described in words)*	White
Soul	SHANTI	Stark wind	Yellow
Etheric	BAJU	Humming of bees	Gold
Mental	MANA	Flowing of water	Blue
Causal	AUM (OM)	Ringing of little bells	Purple or violet
Astral	KALA	Ocean breeze	Rose/Pink
Physical	ALAYA	Thunderstorm	Green

(next page) Illustration of the levels of consciousness that Souls travel through. Chart from Anja Schäfer.

You can download this illustration in color from **venus-spirit.com**.

There is a beautiful meditation CD/download from Omnec Onec available called "Soul Journey" with sounds, mantras and music composed under Venusian Guidance. For more infos see recommendations at the end of this book.

Image 15: Chart "The Godworlds / Levels of Consciousness"

Chapter 18 – Venus Ambassadors Omnec and Cosmic Ray

As I was born on the planet Venus in another dimension and came to your planet as a young child, I was able to retain the knowledge and information that I had gathered as a Soul through many incarnations and life times. I can keep this information intact, and what I teach people is actually what I KNOW and not what I've read about or what I've heard, but what I have experienced through many different life cycles on Earth and in other dimensions.

– Omnec Onec

Planet Earth is currently undergoing a dimensional ascension. In order for Earth's inhabitants to move along with the transformation process, they must expand their consciousness by raising their own vibration.

– Dr. Raymond Keller "Cosmic Ray"

I dedicate this chapter with love and gratitude to my friends and teachers Omnec Onec and Dr. Raymond Keller, also known as "Cosmic Ray". I hope that these lines will inspire you to read their works and watch their videos, because in the videos another quality of their loving, calm presence comes across than through studying their books. I myself have always fed myself in multiple ways throughout my life with the energies that resonated with me; and therefore, I am also very happy and grateful for modern technology with its possibilities of multimedia.

Think for a moment about the time before technologization, when people had only personal contact with each other. Later came the possibility of reading, but that already required education; and because of the patriarchal system, and in many countries also the belief systems that withheld education from women – I'm thinking of the movie *Yentl* with Barbra Streisand, where she dressed up as a young man in order to be able to study – reading and writing was not open to all people. And when people could read and write, they often didn't have unlimited access to all sources of knowledge and to everything that really interested them. The dark ages really did a great job of keeping incarnate Souls down, controlling consciousness and keeping them captive."

Thankfully, this is now coming to an end; and that's why it's so super important to really open up to the light and truth, and to open up the inner gates so that light and love can rise again.

This is exactly why Omnec Onec, Dr. Raymond Keller and very many other great Souls are on Earth right now. I feel infinitely blessed and grateful to have met these wonderful people and thanks to their presence in my life, I have been able to remember so much and continue to grow and thrive.

Ultimately, of course, it is my own Soul, that is, myself, that has chosen and managed all of these experiences in interplay with the other Souls and the divine whole. The more I give space to my self-empowerment, the clearer this truth also becomes, namely that all thanks are also due to myself, because I am all that. Only in this life I have chosen to incarnate myself into a field of oblivion with the option to awaken at a particular point in the course of my life. Perhaps it was, and is, even more than an option. It is rather a life plan that will be fulfilled. I never resisted this either; but my own entanglements with the established system, my own ego and my own wounds had to be confronted. Of course, I could not simply awaken and since then shine forth as a light figure like the "Fool" depicted on the Tarot card as a vagabond or sitting under a Bodhi tree – that was not my life plan. My life plan is to gradually expand my consciousness, for which I encounter new triggers at cyclical intervals that expand me into further dimensions of my consciousness.

Two of these triggers in my life were people, namely Omnec Onec and Dr. Raymond Keller, and one of these triggers was an artifact, namely the already described Phaistos Disc. There is another trigger for the next phase of my awakening, and that is the self-realization coming through the encounter with my twin flame. I write about the subject of twin flames in the last chapter of this book as the crowning icing on the cake.

It is not my intention here to write biographies about Omnec and Ray, I just want to introduce them to you from my personal experience and perspective.

Especially about Omnec, our getting to know each other and her drastic impact on my life I have already written quite extensively. Of course, there is infinitely more to tell. I could tell many stories, and perhaps that shall happen in the future. But, if you want to remember the trigger for writing this book: I am writing it from the possible perspective of a kind of final act before a larger transformation, whatever that may be. It was my initial thought, the pondering about what I would still want to do if I knew that I would only be here on Earth for a few more months. Triggered by this thought, I am writing this book here during my stay in Turkey, which ends tomorrow.

Summarized in short form, so that I get a good transition between Omnec, the woman from Venus and Ray, the man from Venus: Omnec Onec as a person, as a bringer of divine unconditional love and as a spiritual teacher was my main source of information for my path of awakening between 1994 and 2021, when I first met Ray virtually through Facebook Messenger.

In other words, I intuitively always knew that Omnec and her life story were authentic, and I also knew that the spiritual teachings she conveyed were pure and true in essence, albeit packaged via Omnec as a very ordinary human being in a form that was reasonably manageable and digestible, i.e., not overly complicated, albeit very complex.

This background meant for me that I never actively sought out other sources of information or wanted to compare what I knew from Omnec. When I did come into contact with other teachings and teachers, it was always as a supplement, or because I personally needed something specific for my own healing path, such as reading books from the Ascended Master Saint Germain, learning meditation practices, absolving healer trainings, and more.

But when I came in contact with something that was obviously against Omnec and their teachings, that didn't feel coherent to me and I refrained from it.

Of course, there were and are many people for whom Omnec is a fake, a person who just made up her story or who was suffering from some overactive imagination. In particular, I remember a book by an astrologer with whom I had signed up for training and from whom I distanced myself after seeing an image of Omnec in one of his books with an accompanying text that spoke of Neptunian delusion. In other words, this teacher saw Omnec as a dream bubble and all the people who listened to her were under the illusion of the planetary energy of Neptune. When I read that, I knew I had no business being with this astrologer and wrote an email withdrawing my previous registration for a seminar series with him.

Image 16: Dr. Raymond Keller "Cosmic Ray" and Omnec Onec.
The "Historian of the Venusians" and the "Ambassador of the Venusians" met for the first time in 2018 at the Mount Shasta Summer Conference.

The special thing Omnec brought into my life was love, unconditional love. Triggered by the realization of this divine love and my first self-realization, I feel in retrospect, I was really set in my ways for this life; that is, I found my track and knew from that time on that my being here follows a plan and that everything has a purpose, even if I can't always see it right away.

Omnec's love in my life gave me the pool to swim in. Before that, there was no such thing. Before that, I had no idea and was just floating around searching, perhaps like a small fish in a vast ocean that has gotten lost and is somehow looking for its home again.

Through Omnec's presence in my life, this little fish suddenly knew that there was a home and that there were other related fish in similar situations. My whole field of experience began to slowly come into some order.

I learned so much from Omnec, but perhaps it is more accurate to say that through her I remembered a great deal that had always been with me, but which I had forgotten. If you read her books and listen to her words, that is, if Venusian spirituality resonates with you, then you will surely have similar experiences and rediscover many things that you only suspected but now find a certainty of.

This is how it has been not only for me, but for a great many people, that through Omnec's teachings and presence they have found confirmation of what they have always felt, namely the reality of extraterrestrial life, multiple dimensions, a loving Creator, the wonderful power of love as the only reality, and creative imagination as the key to creating reality. The journey of self-discovery has practically taken off in my life through Omnec. At her side and strengthening her back, my role and function as an assistant and as a mouthpiece for her formed more and more, not only in German-speaking countries, but since 2014 also more and more internationally, because that was when we were together for the first time in Norway at a UFO conference.

Only since I met Dr. Raymond Keller in 2021, who brought a new dimension of Venus into my life and, in turn, opened new inner universes for me, did I slowly begin to realize that I am also in a kind of training facilitated by Venusians. It was correct for me to support Omnec, and I still do; but since the time of her stroke in 2009, she withdrew more and more from the public and more and more it crystallized in my consciousness that probably, for the rest of my life, I would have the function to guard and pass on her teachings as best I could.

I mean that the integration of this knowledge and its application is a long process. It is not an education that one completes in one or two years and then one is a trained master of the subject. This is how Earthly training works; but to become a master you need a lot of experience and a lot of practice.

In a different dimension and yet comparable runs a training to a Venus facilitator or ambassador, because it is a real path of spiritual mastery.

I was introduced to Dr. Raymond Keller by two friends, namely Robert Potter, am early and loyal follower of Omnec Onec, who through me had his first private session with her via Skype in 2014. Rob had known about her book for ages and wanted to meet her in person. Rob also organizes the Mount Shasta Summer Conferences where Omnec has attended twice so far, once in 2015 with me and once in 2018 where she was with her daughter Tobi and where she also met Ray for the first time.

The other friend I have not yet met in person, but who has kept in touch for years and who had also helped me proofread my English book "Simply Wisdom and Love – Venusian Spirituality" is Brad Markus.

Rob and Brad occasionally mentioned to me that I really needed to read Ray's books. As I had indicated earlier,

I had been spiritually-Venusian saturated for decades and paid little attention to these prompts from Brad and Rob.

But since they kept talking about Ray, one day I had to take a closer look and suddenly, on impulse, I wrote to Ray via Facebook Messenger. I introduced myself briefly, sent along the photo of Omnec and I from our early days in my bookstore, and really just said "Hello." Ray quickly responded totally, sweetly and interestedly, and a connection was formed between us that soon led to our first acquaintance via Zoom.

During this first conversation, Ray mentioned to me that he had been stationed in Donzdorf near Göppingen as a young man and would love to come back to Germany again. Also, when I asked him about his own Venus experience, he told me that it had been physical, which astonished me very much and also made me curious, because up to that point I had only the information from Omnec that there would be life on the astral plane on Venus, but nothing was known to me about the physical plane.

But I felt the same thing with Ray as I did with Omnec from the beginning, which was his authenticity. I just knew he was telling the truth, or at least a truth that resonated with me.

More conversations arose between Ray and I and quickly we decided together that he would come to Germany, which led me to the next question, which is that we have nothing to offer from him in German, neither a video, nor a book, nor a text, nothing.

My first idea was to write my own little book about Venus, a kind of summary or something like that, because when Ray sent me his first book "Venus Rising – A Concise History of the Second Planet" and I started to read it, I already suspected that this would be a huge task to translate this book into German and I searched in myself for an alternative solution; but I did not find it.

In view of Ray's planned trip to Germany in May 2022 and the fact that I wanted to organize a small tour with lectures for him, I had about half a year to plan the events and to publish a book. When I was in Spain for a few weeks in the fall of 2021, I thought all the time about a solution to this dilemma and finally decided that I would not be able to cope with writing my own book at that time, so that I would like to have Ray's first book translated into German and published on the occasion of his visit to Germany.

Image 17: Cosmic Ray and I in Salzburg, Austria.

One of our Venus presentations durung our beautiful "From Venus with Love Tour 2022". You can watch the recordings on my YouTube channel @ venus-spirit.

With this decision, my training as a Venus facilitator entered the next phase. The work on this book turned out to be my personal doctoral thesis and this was related to all kinds of factors, not only the scope and the language, but there were also enormous organizational and technical components, some of which I almost failed at. In a very short time, I had to go through a new training in Word, in matters of layout with InDesign, in communication with proofreaders, in copyright matters, in questions of image material and its use, and then also purely energetically, because the energy in Ray's books is for me personally in a frequency that leads my whole consciousness into a new dimension of remembering and awakening. In parallel, I organized the tour, which led me into a new dimension of networking with people, both in terms of regional organizers and potential visitors – in that sense, I also had much more in terms of communication and immersion with people than in the decades before. It brought me, overall, into a new level of connections and exchanges; and I met many new people and connected on a new level with some I had known on the fringes for a long time, but who suddenly stepped closer into my field of consciousness through these months of activities and planning. I also met some new people and made new connections. In all of this, there was a lot more. For example, a new website was created during this preparation time for Ray's visit, I started translating articles by Ray for the *UFO Nachrichten* newspaper.

I could tell you so much more about the intense months working with Ray, but from the pure perspective of his presence in my life, after decades of pure Omnec energy, I can summarize by saying that for me he transports a male Venus component, while Omnec brought the female Venus component. These are only terms that certainly cannot represent the full truth, they only tentatively describe the many dimensions of my experience.

Perhaps it helps a little if I say that Omnec has primarily carried the spiritual teaching, the love, the essence of the spiritual, and Ray has primarily carried the scientific, the history, the connection of the spiritual with the physical through his enormous research, his seven intensive books and numerous articles to date; and all of this is interwoven with his own experiences of awakening including his own stay on Venus for 10 weeks.

Both Omnec and Ray are for me personally two of the gentlest, most loving, wisest Souls I have met in my narrow field; and I say that deliberately because there are, of course, other loving, wise Souls. Some of them I recognize as true teachers, whose works I love to read and whose voices I love to hear, but they are all not as closely connected to me in my own life as Omnec and Ray, both of whom are absolute representatives of Venus and its messengers, and with whom I am in regular, intimate, friendly exchange.

With Ray's entry into my life, a new chapter clearly began on the path of my own spiritual development. Not only did his presence and knowledge give me a huge boost in new insights and experiences – added to this was the beginning of the completion of my ascension process through the encounter with my twin flame. I write about this special "road of awakening" in the last chapter of this book.

Now – as it is known that there are no coincidences, but only Soul appointments and Soul plans, it becomes more and more clear that I have chosen exactly these two teachers as a connecting field between Omnec and Ray, in order to awaken into my full consciousness and to embody and pass on Venusian spirituality myself from some point on.

Maybe I'm even doing that already, but I don't feel fully awakened at the moment; I definitely still feel turbulence – but maybe that's also completely human and simply a sign of this time of transformation, that Souls on the path of awakening are also confronted with challenges and don't rest completely, deeply relaxed serene in their center within every breath. After all, it is also about the clearing of the lower bodies and frequencies. It is also about the dissolution of bonds and about the healing of the primordial trauma as a result of the separation from the Divine that took place upon entry on Earth's material plane of existence. This is not done in the twinkling of an eye, but is a process.

Image 18: With Ray at the famous Untersberg mountain.
This photo was taken on June 5, 2022, at the foot of the Untersberg mountain in Austria during an excursion with a small group.

As I write these lines, I am looking into the last hours of my stay in Turkey. From my hotel room window, I see clouds and a clearing sky after a lot of rain for several days. I hear the beautiful music of Gioari's "Mountain of Illumination" – fitting the theme I just wrote about. In the two weeks I've been here, I've feasted quite a bit. The sweets here at the hotel are the absolute bomb, even better than all the other food which is also very good. But the cakes and treats – blatantly tempting – I'm glad that's over again tomorrow when I'm back in Germany.

With these words I close this chapter; and if you want to dive deeper into the teachings and energies of the wonderful Souls Omnec Onec and Dr. Raymond Keller, then check out the recommendations in the back of the book, there are also playlists on my YouTube channel with videos with the two.

The experience of the individual heaven does not depend on what the human being has achieved or not achieved during his life, but on how much he has opened himself to the infinite love of the divine presence. God is love and just like the Earth, the more developed Venus is a part of the divine plan and the heavenly kingdom.

As Earth's sister planet, Venus supports man's inner ascension through its harmonious radiation, which it continuously sends to Earth and into the hearts of men.

Even the seeming small is significant.

– Dr. Raymond Keller "Cosmic Ray"

Chapter 19 – Omnec's Oasis

The Oasis is a place of the future, supported by everyone working together. A place that will endure long after the transformation of the Earth. It will be a place of love and support and respect for all living beings, as the Creator intended.

– Omnec Onec

Image 19: Main house of Omnec's Oasis.

Omnecs Oasis – A Place in Harmony with the Universe. Drawing based on a vision by Anja Schäfer.

Omnec and I ceased to actively work for the realization of the Oasis[13] along with her last trip to Germany in 2016. She received the information from her Venusian guidance that the project is completed on the higher realms.

For the manifestation on the physical Earth, we will have to be aligned in divine timing, that means, all those of us who are somehow connected with this project will be contacted when the time is right. So since 2016, I have not talked or written about this project in public. For this book however, I would like to revive this beautiful subject, because we are still in the middle of the transformation and I feel it's of high importance to give a lot of love and attention to positive visions. Even if the concrete realization of the Oasis, as we have envisioned it, still belongs to the realm of utopia and thus definitely to the fifth-dimensional Earth, into which we are just entering and which is coming towards us at lightspeed, I feel it's fun and playful to give energy to beautiful visions like this one. Because: Imagination is the key to Creation!

It is interesting that I choose this terminology right now, because at the end of the nineties, when I received the Oasis vision, I did not think or speak in these 5D-terms yet, but now I have a better understanding. I also better understand why Omnec said that the Oasis will not be manifested until the transformation of the Earth is complete. Having realized this, we "had to stop" active work on the project in 2016, because the timing wasn't right. All further efforts at that point would have been fruitless.

It was a special blessing which Omnec received returning on her way from the USA to Germany and which she passed on to us. During our last Oasis meeting, she revealed to us that the Oasis would be finished on a higher level.

13 All Omnec's Oasis illustrations and texts are online on **https://omnec-onec.com/omnecs-oasis/**

Looking back, I believe that most of the people who were actively involved in the Oasis team at that time did not find this blessing as deeply gratifying as I did. I had the feeling that most of them were disappointed and that in their eyes it seemed that we have given up on continuing to work on the manifestation of Omnec's Oasis.

From my perspective the blessing allowed us to hand the project over to the divine and to the higher forces of manifestation until the time is right for it's realization on the physical Earth. So to say: "Let go - and let God!"

The creation of the means and the Earthly conditions was neither possible for me nor for the team with conventional 3D measures and it also did not feel like my task to be active in a way that did not correspond to my Soul's plan. I was pulled away, so to speak, to devote myself to other things and that was also totally coherent and a huge relief. Nevertheless, I needed the blessing of letting go, because the Oasis project had started to become a burden for me, but at the same time I felt the beauty and the importance of this project – that's why I was in a dilemma for a while. Omnec solved this dilemma with the blessing from above, and I surrendered.

With the visualization and the beginning of the groupings around this vision, I was very committed to the Oasis for several years. In 2016, the Oasis Project had gathered enough subtle material around it, so to speak, through thoughts, wishes, feelings, and visualizations. Everything else was and is in God's plan and no longer in our hands. I believe the Oasis will gradually get closer to the Earth with the increase of its vibration. The Oasis and similar projects of this kind come towards us from the subtle world and we go further towards it by raising our own frequency.

I am including the vision and information about this project here, although I have already published it in our book "Simply Wisdom and Love – Venusian Spirituality". The Oasis texts and illustrations are also published on Omnec Onec's website.

I still love this vision very much, and I believe it is worth it that it may find its way once again to some more hearts and vision bearers, so this way it may get a new push towards manifestation.

Omnec invites all people to participate in the Oasis Project

In 1992, Omnec visited the Hancock Building in Chicago with a friend from Germany. They were speaking of Unarius, the Universal School in California, where people come to study past life experiences and are preparing a university of extraterrestrial teachings.

Omnec told her friend that she would like to also teach Universal teachings and have such a school. Enjoying their amazing view and their light humorous atmosphere, they thought and talked of ideas and concepts in connection with this spontaneous idea.

Omnec says that her Uncle Odin passed on the following message to her: "Omnec, you will establish such a place for all to share knowledge and receive spiritual truth. You have created it by visualizing this place. It should be a safe place but not identified with the concepts of schools or religions of Earth."

Then, the word "Oasis" came into Omnec's mind and she felt such a joy, because she understood that an oasis is almost the same and has such a wonderful meaning. Later, she saw the word "Oasis" everywhere: "Oasis Travel," Oasis Restaurant," Oasis Esoteric Store," etc. Omnec thought she had to think of something else! Then Fubbi and Rebazar [two of her masters] said: "Omnec's Oasis!"

Omnec said: "What? Why me?"

"Because your teachings are known for truth from the first humans, and they are about Soul, the real essence of life".

Omnec was excited then and couldn't wait to share this information with her friend. He said "No, it shall not have your name! How egotistical!"

She said to him: "Yes, Oasis is good".

Later on, Omnec told her close friends about this idea, and they said: "How will anyone know that it isn't just a restaurant or store? This place should have your name!"

From then on, Omnec spoke publicly to people at workshops about the idea for "Omnec's Oasis."

This letter from Omnec that follows here was written in early 2001, when we first wrote to all the people who were in the Omnec Onec address database at the time:

I would like to invite all who are interested to contribute to Omnec's Oasis. It is to be a Spiritual Center not based on a particular teaching but to encompass all.
It will not exclude or support any particular religion, race, or culture but give all a chance to express themselves as an individual or group.
The doors shall always be open – on a 24 hour basis with someone always there to share time ore give you the feeling of acceptance.
You may receive or give from your particular circumstance.
Of course, you will have to contribute either money or time to attend to certain duties to maintain the Oasis.
There will be a music room with instruments and sound system, or you may bring your own musical instrument.
There will be a meditation room and also a place to eat, or drink and smoke. If you need solitude, this is possible.

There will be many types or healings available as well as scheduled topics and workshops. Or course, you may bring sleeping bags or rent a room for sleeping. No reservation necessary.
There will be provided guidelines or ethics which shall be upheld.
The sign over the entrance shall state YOU ARE NOT JUDGED HERE.
Art and sculptures will be displayed or created here also. Here you can express yourself or share your talents with others. It will be a place of combined efforts belonging to all who wish to contribute.
It is the place of the future supported by co-operation.
A place that will stand long after the transformation. A place of love and support and respect of all living entities as the Creator intended.
If you wish to support this or raise funds with a special project it shall be appreciated.
I of course will be there at appointed times.
Thank you for your support of my mission on this planet Earth.
Love and Blessings
Omnec

Anja's Oasis Vision Texts

I wrote the following vision texts in 2006, when I created the first Oasis website. Please consider these texts as a whole as impulses and "spiritual seeds". They are received from an inner level and left in their original form except for basic corrections.

Where repetitions occur, they are intentional to enhance the energy and deepen the visualization.

Oasis Vision

The Oasis is a place in complete harmony with nature.

In the Oasis, people may live, work and stay as long as they'd like. The Oasis is open 24 hours a day for visitors and people in need of a place to rest and recover.

In the Oasis, peace and calmness rule as a natural state. There are also a variety of events taking place on a regular basis. Everything here is voluntary, but there are some simple rules and guidelines.

The Oasis is a place of balanced giving and taking. Every visitor, guest and inhabitant contributes in whatever way is possible and comfortable for them. The inner order of the Oasis is maintained through the natural intuition of the people there and through meetings of the people who are living there and wish to take part. In these meetings, all points are discussed which are to be addressed, as well as important decisions made.

In the Oasis, the "Communication of the Heart" is relied upon. That means, every person may speak what is on their mind while the others listen.

A central theme of the Oasis is "You are not judged here". Love and acceptance replace judgement and criticism.

The foundation of the Oasis is the Earth itself. Life in the Oasis pulses in harmony with the Earth and is protected and supported by it. The care and maintenance of the Oasis is also in harmony with nature.

The place as a whole offers room for peace, healing, creativity, and learning.

The gardens are full of beauty and are used for the planting and cultivation of fruits and vegetables, flowers and herbs.

The core of the Oasis are people who are living naturally and in harmony with the ideals upon which the Oasis is based. All subjects concerning the daily life in the Oasis are directed by this core. No matter what question emerges, it is discussed by the core; that means the heart of the Oasis is asked, just as every individual in the Oasis asks their own heart for guidance. For those who don't ask the heart for guidance first, it is possible they may therefore not feel comfortable at the Oasis for any extended time, due to a lack of overall resonance.

The heart of the Oasis is a powerful energy that is in harmony with the Earth and the movement of our solar system. This place is a safe place in the holistic sense, in that it grows and develops in accordance with the nature of the times.

The essence of the Oasis is its harmonious energy in which healing, happiness, and peace can be.

The Oasis is built on an acupuncture point of the Earth's surface. Other places like this already exist, are being built right now, and with more to come in the future. All these places of peace, healing, and harmony are connected along the Earth's meridians. In this way, a powerful net of protection is built which also stabilizes the Earth while helping to raise its vibrations.

Oasis Grounds

The place where the Oasis is situated is spacious and open, but comfortable.

The Oasis consists of a main house, a living house, apartments/bungalows, a place for animals and a camping area.

All houses are connected by foot paths which are mostly covered by sand.

Between the houses are gardens and open green spaces.

There is a lake near the camping area. A small river flows close by the living house, the animal house and the bungalows.

In front of the main house there is a large circular patch of grass with flowers surrounding a fountain.

There is a parking area before the entrance to the Oasis property. The Oasis itself remains auto-free. The only cars and big machines in the Oasis are the ones that are necessary for work or transportation purposes.

The Oasis is only accessible to the world of streets in the front. Nature surrounds the Oasis otherwise, including forest, fields, and open space. One can see mountains rising up in the distance.

All the houses are built in an organic style with an emphasis on curves not corners, and this style is continued inside the buildings. In this way, the buildings create a soft and friendly environment. There are also columns and covered areas outside.

The main building of the Oasis is beautiful. Wide gentle steps lead up to the main entrance here. The outside is constructed with columns and invites one to relax and enjoy the view looking out over the round of green and fountain bubbling in the center as well as to feel the peace emanating from the environment.

The entrance is high and rounded. As far as the weather allows it, the doors are open.

There is a big circular mosaic of colored glass above the main entrance door. Above it are letters that convey the meaning of the heart of the Oasis. Underneath is the word Oasis written in the same style of letters. This script used here are thought forms which transcend the meaning of written language.

Inside the Oasis is a round area decorated with plants and water. Above, the space is open with many plants growing, some all the way to the roof. The roof is open but can be closed during cold or wet weather as necessary.

The main house is three stories. On the first floor left is a café/restaurant with an al fresco area. To the right, also opening to the outside, is a business with books and crystals and all kinds of related accessories. Integrated into the business is a large area for reading and relaxing where drinks and fruit are freely available.

To the back from the main entrance area is a larger room with a stage for the presentation of various events and music.

All together the interior of the Oasis is flooded with light, full of wonderful plants, and water bubbles gently all around. There is a sense of peace and lightness. A great staircase sweeps up into the second floor.

There is an open landing full of plants that also allows a view onto the main first floor. It is very open and light. The large plants and trees grow from below on the first floor, right past, and up to the roof.

Here are many "color rooms". The "color rooms" are variously furnished and each in a different lovely color. For example, there is a purple room, which is completely purple and in which there are magnificent amethysts as well as a few pictures and decorations that go with the purple theme.

Furthermore, there is a blue room, a green room, an orange room, as well as a yellow room, a turquoise room, a pink room and finally the rainbow room. Unfortunately, not all colors and shades can be represented in the physical, so the core has to decide which colors are currently on display.

The color rooms are available for creative and healing purposes but also open for simple enjoyment. All the rooms have some sort of outer access, like a balcony, which usually includes a lovely view.

Another set of beautiful stairs leads up to the top floor and meditation room.

The meditation room is a dome made of white color, glass, and light.

Here the meetings of the core of the Oasis take place, as well as regular meditations. At all other times, this special room is open for the enjoyment of all.

There is a terrace on the roof full of plants and offering many seating areas.

Besides the main entrance, the main house of the Oasis has three other doors in each of the cardinal directions.

To the left and behind the main house one finds the big living house.

On the ground floor of the living house is a kitchen, dining room, an office, and a large walk-in pantry.

In the upper three floors there are numerous rooms, where permanent citizens of the Oasis as well as guests are living.

Behind the big living house are bungalows. The bungalows are round and sitting on stilts.

All rooms and bungalows can be decorated and adjusted to meet the needs of the people living in them.

To the left and the front of the main house, is a garden where food is grown as well as a house and place for animals.

There are a variety of animals that call the Oasis home, and how their living area looks can be changed or adjusted according to needs.

The people communicate with the heart of the animals so that their wishes and needs are met as well as those of the people.

To the right of the main house is a camping house and area on the shore of a small lake. There are many trees.

The camping house contains all the necessities for living in the camping area. This area of the Oasis is available for all those who enjoy living in a tent or camper or otherwise enjoy living close to nature.

The entire Oasis is crisscrossed by footpaths which connect all houses with each other and lead in various directions into nature.

This description of the Oasis represents just one possibility. The picture is not fixed but changeable according to the emotions, thoughts, and actions of the people whose vision its realization reflects.

Through conversations and collaborative visualization at the Oasis project meetings that took place until 2016, several new homes and areas of the Oasis site have been added:

- A playground for different ages in the neighborhood of the animal area
- A separate area for horses and healing work with horses and people
- A house for inventions and development of new technologies. Research laboratory
- A house for celebrations with stage, dance floor and music system
- A creative house for artistic design and exhibitions
- A section of garden for fairies and elves as an invitation for the settlement by nature beings (respectful treatment, entering only signposted paths allowed).
- A second residential building, which connects both residential buildings, which are like twin houses, via a roof bridge.
- The individual residences at the rear of the Oasis site are allowed to be very different – the stilt houses indicated on this original illustration are for illustrative purposes.

Oasis Realization

The realization of the Oasis is possible.

According to the motto "Imagination is the key to creation," everything can be realized that one can imagine.

The Oasis is a place of the heart and of peace. It emerges through the power of imagination of many peaceful hearts. The attention of the people who love this place enable it to become reality.

No person alone could ever create the Oasis, even if the financial means were available. The Oasis is a project that results from combined energies and efforts. All the people who dream of this place, who long for this place, who wish for this place, send their energy into the heart of the Oasis. Out of the heart this project grows and gathers to it the necessary material. In this way the Oasis is grounded and realized. It is literally created and takes root naturally.

The spirit of the Oasis exists as a vision of planet Earth itself. The Earth is a beautiful planet that lovingly supports all life forms. The Earth is longing for peace and appreciation through its citizens. The development and being of places like the Oasis is wished.

The spirit of the Oasis exists in the ether and is received by numerous people. From here the Oasis finds entrance through the heart.

These people are filled with a vision like this, dream of it, and imagine a place and life which they fill with their joy and energy.

The next step towards realizing this vision is sharing it with other through words and pictures.

Step by step the hearts of the people who share this vision are connected and exchange information contributing to its further growth and development.

The heart of the Oasis collects more and more energy and starts to pulse in resonance with the Earth and therefore continues to grow.

Somewhere, sometime the Oasis is real, lives on the Earth in the physical dimension and is connected with other places of this kind.

This net contributes to the development of Earth towards a light and loving vibration that is harmonious with the Universe.

Chapter 20 – From Venus with Love

When you have experienced love in all its facets, you come to know unconditional love.

Venus love is unconditional love.

– Omnec Onec

So much can be said about love and in truth nothing can be said about it at all. That is why in this chapter I relate what I have heard from Omnec Onec about love and pass it on from the point of view of Venusian spirituality, as it was conveyed to me in the voice of a Venusian whose Soul consciousness has always been unclouded and undivided and who therefore has access to the truth of creation in a special clarity.

The Creator, that is, God, the Sugmad, the Unity Consciousness, the source of all that is, loved Himself so much that He created everything that is from within Himself, because in this way He will never cease to exist. Love is the foundation of creation and never ceases; in fact, there is nothing other than love. God, the source, created and continues to create Souls in infinite cycles, sparks of light that are made of the same material as Himself. Thus, God continues to exist and unfold forever, because through the Souls that make their journeys through the levels of consciousness, God experiences Himself.

I know that this is a very simplified explanation of the divine and the Souls. It has always been Omnec's endeavor and also her talent to convey the great interrelationships of creation in very simple words and pictures. This talent was given to her by her masters so that she could reach the Souls embodied on Earth whom she was supposed to reach and who, viewed the other way around, resonate with Omnec's voice.

Fortunately, Omnec's mission on Earth has been successful through her existence in the sense that she has survived and shared her complete message of love and truth through her books and personal contacts.

It is now up to us, who feel resonant with this energy, with this teaching and with these words, to internalize the knowledge in our own lives and to carry it forward through our presence.

One could also express it in such a way that Omnec was brought to Earth as a child with her full consciousness in order to bring pure love, unadulterated, uncompromised, above all, unshadowed by her own forgetfulness. And through herself, she ignites the sparks in the hearts of the still sleeping Souls in order to make them blaze.

In a sense, there is definitely a similarity here to the presence of Christ, for although he naturally reached many more Souls on Earth, the question has remained after thousands of years as to how many of them really made love blossom in their hearts in its pure form, lived it and passed it on.

The shadow of the darkening of human consciousness on Earth lay heavy and still does today, although through the great transformation of the Earth much more light is already streaming through the cloud cover and much more truth and love has already spread in human hearts. The realm of experience of the third-dimensional reality is a discontinued model, its time is coming to an end and this is possibly the truth behind the end of many old calendars.

The process of illuminating and loving human Souls is irreversible, for it is God's plan that the Earth be restored to its original purpose, and that is to be a paradise where divine love is omnipresent.

Omnec has always called it that the Earth is a jewel and that it was an immense undertaking of very many loving, great Souls from different directions of the galaxies to populate this beautiful planet with life of various forms. Earth is meant to be a symbol, a living library of many facets of life and life forms. This was and is its original purpose of existence, to which it is now being returned by the great transformation. For this, it must be freed from all the shadows and negative forces that have imprisoned the embodied Souls on Earth in great unconsciousness for thousands of years. This was allowed in God's plan for the experiences of the Souls, because there is nothing outside of God's plan, but there is maximum oblivion and maximum separation from God consciousness within creation.

As I mentioned in the chapter about the cycles and timelines with the two current directions of development, at the moment there are these two ways for which the Souls can decide: Either in the ascent of consciousness towards fifth-dimensional (or higher) existence or in the descent of consciousness towards two-dimensional (or digital, artificial) existence.

There are different opinions and ideas about what will happen to the Earth itself. Some believe there will be two Earths. Omnec has described it in such a way that the negative forces will leave the Earth, because they are not in resonance with the frequency of the higher, warm light and therefore do not fit here from the vibration any more. According to Omnec, the Souls who have the choice with which direction of development they wish to make their further experiences will also leave the old Earth and "recycle", i.e. make their transition back into the spiritual world, in order to reincarnate later with a new body in which the expanded consciousness has room. Whether this will be exactly so or whether we on the Earth similarly as on Venus simply have the life in several frequency levels at the same time, what many experience as now already, we will see. Maybe every individual really experiences it in the same way as he creates the experience for himself and this in harmony with related Souls. Many are already experiencing the dimensional blends, time jumps and synchronicities that are a sign of the penetration of higher dimensions. Also invisibilities, when one vibrates in a totally different frequency than the environment and one is not perceived at all or does not perceive others who vibrate much lower, occur more and more.

However, each individual experiences this phase of the Earth's vibrational shift, the key to experiencing this journey in peace, joy, serenity, humor and with all the bliss and wonder is – yes, what is the key? It is perhaps best that you define it for yourself.

From my point of view, signs like "serendipity" and the measure of inner peace are part of recognizing what is just right and where I am on my Soul journey. I find that the alignment with one's own heart and the inherent love is always and without exception the right way – as well as the sharing and sharing of love.

Venus Love is Unconditional Love

Unconditional love is a term that is meaningless if it has no meaning for you. Besides, it sounds different in every language – the language itself can always transport only one energy at a time. The moment a word comes out of the mouth, it is already in the dual world and is therefore often interpreted differently, misunderstood or not heard at all.

Terms like love and God mean very different things to very many people. And those who do not understand the language do not understand the words.

Nevertheless, every human being understands energies, because all human beings are in truth energy beings. They are only encased in biological bodies, in organisms, but through these bodies vibrates the energy of the essence of that which inhabits that body.

When this inner being is in unclouded resonance with its Creator, who is nothing but love, then this energy automatically resonates out and back in through the denser bodies into its experiential world.

Love your neighbor as yourself. This is what is meant by this, because in truth it is all one – the neighbor and I are apparently two, but in the inner planes they are not, in the inner planes the neighbor and I are one. And that is why God dwells in one's own heart and never anywhere outside, God is the neighbor who is one with me and who I am.

In order to recognize this truth deep within oneself, and not just to think or believe, an inner Soul realization, a remembrance, a realization is needed.

When and in which way this kind of realization finds a person is in his Soul plan. But just reading spiritual literature and listening to the words of real masters brings these levels of truth to sound and leads to the realizations.

By unconditional love, Omnec means the absolute acceptance of everything that is. To love as God loves, that is what is meant. And God as the Creator created everything that is out of love, so He also loves everything equally and without distinction. To realize this love consciousness in the human body is almost inconceivable for many people because we usually discriminate, that is part of the dual field of experience. We differentiate into what we like and love and what we dislike. This distinction is from my point of view also absolutely correct and human and it is an expression of love to myself, if I have the intention and pay attention that I surround myself in my life with everything I love and value and let go more and more in love what in truth burdens me or what I simply do not like.

But behind that there is another level and that is meant here by unconditional love. That is, everything is as it is right now. That is the acceptance of the actual state. In relation to other people, it means that I love and accept the Soul in the other person because it is a part of God, just as I, as a Soul, am a part of God. It is no more and no less than this that is meant by unconditional love – it is the recognition of the living Soul in the other, even in the animal and in the plant and in the mineral and in all forms of life that I do not perceive with my physical senses. It is the recognition of their existence as something that was created by the Creator and that is therefore loved – loved on the level of unity, of unity consciousness.

That does not mean that I have to agree to everything in my life situations or that I have to like everything. Every form is subject to change or to dissolve – even a relationship form or a thought form. I don't have to say yes to everything – quite the opposite. Love for myself means that I set boundaries, that I feel exactly what feels right for me and what does not. A boundary can also be set in love. Anything, also a partnership or a professional, friendly, religious or family situation can be changed or ended in love.

The recognition of the God Presence as my true nature, the essence of who I am and the level in which I am really and truly one with all created and uncreated, that is, from my understanding, being in love.

Omnec Onec is for me personally the master teacher in matters of divine love, because I have known her personally for decades and have experienced many things together with her. I know from my own experience how it feels to live unconditional love from the high consciousness of a Soul living here among us.

And through my own first initiation into the experience of unconditional love, which I have already mentioned in a few places in this book, I know how it feels to pass on a fire of love and what effects it can have in one's own life.

Therefore, all that I write here is told from my own experience and memory and not as a theoretical treatise on love. If from these many words in this book even one spark has jumped into your heart, making your own heart fire a little bigger, then this book has fulfilled more than I could ever have dreamed of.

In the next chapter, which rounds off this book, I will tell you about a road of awakening into divine love that is currently being walked by more and more Souls: the Twin Flames.

Chapter 21 – Twin Flames

To have the Gift of the Highest Love possible and the Glory of my Twin Ray in one who has this marvelous True Understanding is a miracle to me – and a thing I have been craving all my Life!

The happiness of having found the 'Mighty I AM Presence' within myself is beyond words.

– "The Magic Presence," Book 2 of the Saint Germain Series by Godfré Ray King.

That I would once write about this highly spiritual, sacred subject and that too based on my own experience, is something very special for me. I dedicate to the twin flames this last chapter in this story, which has no beginning and no end, because in truth a cycle opens and closes herewith again. Normally, I would say that it is not yet ripe for me to speak about this, but today I rise above my own demands and limitations and say: Yes, it is ripe. The subject of twin flames is a global one and knowledge about it, especially when it is based on personal experience and not just theory, belongs to be spoken out.

I would even say that it is conveyed from learned knowledge and hearsay by probably the fewest people, simply because it belongs to such a highly spiritual level of experience that to those who have not experienced it themselves, it must seem most like science fiction, utopia, wishful thinking or fairy tales, i.e. like something seemingly unattainable, something mystical, something sacred – or something invented. Someone who does not have this experience himself cannot report about it authentically.

The twin flame encounter is an extreme and uncompromisingly fast road of awakening.

It is something sacred. And for that reason, I can't say very much about it yet. The little I share with you in this chapter I write especially for you who feel a resonance with this and perhaps have either already met your twin flame yourself or feel in your heart an inkling that it belongs in your life.

I am deliberately expressing myself very carefully, because I am not sure that all Souls travel through the levels of consciousness as Twin Souls. However, I do believe that those who are traveling as Twin Souls are incarnating more and more in parallel right now in this time of transformation of the Earth to help Mother Earth ascend by bringing a special frequency of love.

But even if the twin flame experience should not belong to your self-chosen field of experience and awakening, you are also a person in whose life topics such as relationships, enlightenment and love play an essential role, otherwise you would not read this book.

Before I delve further into the twin flames, I want to state clearly that there are several roads of awakening; the twin flame road is one of them. All Souls who awaken into their full consciousness have the freedom to complete their reincarnation cycles and, through their awakening alone, help the Earth in its vibrational upliftment and healing.

Although I have already said it in several places in the course of this book, I would like to emphasize it again specifically for this topic that everything I write here is based on personal experience and based on my current state of knowledge and on what feels right for me here and now. Check with your intuition and your heart yourself what of it resonates with you and just discard everything else.

Twin flames are one Soul in two incarnations. They are identical in energy, made of the same frequency material. They come from the same egg of God.

Soul is a spark of God. God is pure love. Thus, Soul is also pure love. Soul without the body of the polar worlds around it is comparable to a drop in the ocean. The ocean corresponds to God, the Creator Source, the divine I AM Presence, the All-that-is. The drop corresponds to the Soul, absolutely identical with its source and at the same time an individualized aspect, especially by deciding to go to the lower, polar worlds and to clothe oneself with a body in each frequency level or dimension in order to have experiences in this dimension. Experiencing oneself through experiences is the reason for traveling through the planes of consciousness. All Souls are complete in themselves, absolutely pure and perfect. They remain so for all eternity; they are whole and holy.

In order to experience in the lower frequency dimensions, some Souls make the decision to split their inherent polarities of divine feminine and divine masculine, which doubles their spectrums of experience. Thus, after descending into the denser worlds, they travel as a pair of Souls that are nevertheless one and always and inseparably connected. It is only seemingly a separation of polarities into yin and yang, male and female, electric and magnetic, with one aspect always present within the other Soul aspect. A Soul is and always remains complete, also when it is traveling through the denser worlds as the divine-feminine or divine-male polarity.

As you can see in the Godworlds illustration, according to our spiritual conception, after the worlds of unity, there is a kind of boundary line, which we call the etheric dimension and which represents the border into the worlds of duality. This is where the decision takes place whether a Soul will begin its experiential journey as a Twin Soul or whether it will remain a unity. This view is of course not set in stone, like nothing I say here, maybe *all* Souls go off as Twin Souls and there are also teachers who say that a Soul can travel in even more aspects than in twos into the planes of experience, because ultimately, presumably, just about anything is possible in this plane, which is so difficult for the little mind incarnated here to grasp and completely certainly not, at least not for me.

I am spreading out this whole carpet to convey to you that I think many things are possible, but I decide here for the variant which I can comprehend and above all which I have experienced myself – and that is the realization of myself as a Soul in another embodiment.

I had always been on an uncompromising quest for ultimate love, and, although I was not consciously aware of it until I was 52 years old, perhaps in retrospect this inner longing indicates that I incarnated as a twin flame. As I have written throughout this book, the fulfillment of this inner longing in terms of a happy love relationship always remained unfulfilled, and each time I fell in love my heart suffered and I collided with a new experience of pain through unrequited and unfulfilled love. On the other hand, it always lifted me spiritually into new dimensions of experience and knowledge – I evolved into greater and greater consciousness through each experience of unrequited love. My life was and is about the dissolution of bonds and about finding the truth, therefore I decided as a Soul not to enter into firm bonds in the old 3D-expiration model. Of course, having been identified with ego-consciousness, thus in unconsciousness, I was unable to understand this for decades.

I always thought there was something wrong with me, so that the happiness of a love relationship was not granted to me. At times I even thought that there was some kind of curse on me and that it was a punishment that I couldn't find a partner and that no man could love me. In innumerable conversations in the course of my life with female friends, through reading books, attending seminars and consulting people from whom I hoped to receive healing and advice, the bottom line came out that I only had to wish for it in the right way or that I had to work on myself or that every pot eventually finds its lid or that I fall in love with the wrong people and that involved making compromises in a partnership and that I was too stubborn and had too high expectations and so on and so forth. Or men were afraid of me because I was so independent and dominant, or it would certainly work out sometime in the future, or it was not so important, I didn't need a man. Sometimes I was also told that my life–long single status was simply uncomprehensible, because I was attractive and intelligent and everything was fine with me. The whole issue was really a lifelong problem until the year 2019, when I arrived at inner peace with being single. I call it "a lifelong problem", because when I look back I realize that I was on the wrong train and docked to the programming that I *need* a partner to have love in my life. In retrospect, it is so obvious that a solution can never be found on this linear level and I am sure many people who – other than I – lived or still live relationships or marriages are often stuck in 3D models of love relationships, in traditional ways of thinking in terms of romantic relationships and in Earth's conditioning of what love is. Very few ever have experienced divine love. This is exactly *one* reason for the transformation of the Earth and the incarnation of twin flames, who experience the high, unconditional love via their heart chakra activation and thus the homecoming into the love of God and bring it to Earth in their bodies. Twin flames are part of the great transformation process that lifts the whole Earth into the wonderful high frequency of the fifth dimensional level of reality, where divine love will finally be a lived reality.

Today I have deep insight into the truth that the belief that love and happiness can be found outside of oneself and the obsessive desire for a partnership are programming of the matrix and consequences of the genetic manipulation of humanity and that the whole man-woman-family theme as we have known it globally for thousands of years needs a transformation of consciousness. I am aware today that I have incarnated as one of the Souls to break down these encrusted structures and to help both myself and people to allow true, divine love to rise within and be embodied. We are here to help Mother Earth, through the homecoming of divine love, to rise to a higher vibrational frequency and end the age of darkness and ignorance.

In retrospect, I see in this whole scenario the drama of indoctrination and programming, which sits deep in the Earthly societies and genes. Any kind of inner or, depending on the societial structures, even outer compulsion to have to find a partner in order to be apparently complete and happy and because this is simply socially or religiously right and a requirement, is wrong and keeps the Souls imprisoned. This program keeps the Souls in bondage and in karmic, often loveless entanglements, because in the rarest cases a couple finds each other and consciously walks the path of awakening and unconditional love together. This was also almost impossible for millennia in the 3D plane of experience – on the contrary – the vibration was so low and dense that true love had almost no space for experience. The incarnation of twin flames was an exception and, in my opinion, always served to bring the special quality of divine love and teaching[14] – just as various masters of wisdom were also sent to Earth by God again and again. Very rarely twin flames were destined to come together and live their Soul love in a lived connection. Furthermore, there are forces which have worked against the incarnation of twin flames for thousands of years and which, when they were incarnated, disturbed and prevented their activation and coming together. These forces are still here today, but they are dwindling and losing their influence – this is one reason why more and more twin flames are coming together. I believe that in the course of the coming years and decades more and more twin flames will also find their way into the lived connection. The higher the frequency of the Earth rises, the more twin flames in harmonious unity it can host – and this is also its intention.

The process of raising the vibration is connected for the incarnated twin flames with a great journey home to themselves. They rise on a fast track from the third dimensional to the fifth dimensional consciousness. This journey, at this time as I write this book, is often still accompanied by periods of outer separation for many after the initial activation. During these outer separation phases, each Soul flame does its inner work for itself in its embodiment, acknowledges and realizes love, completes Soul contracts and find its way into its perfect divine alignment. Time and encounters run in twin flame connections in cyclical, divine time and not in linear time.

The common conscious inner alignment with Source is the key for the lived, harmonious connection.

---

14 I point to the Elizabeth Clare Prophet (1939-2009) and Mark L. Prophet (1918-1973) who found each other as a Twin Flame couple and together founded the Summit Lighthouse movement. There are many videos of Twin Flames lectures on the website **https://www.summitlighthouse.org/** and on YouTube.

Image 20: Twin Flames Illustration.

Credit and gratitude goes to The Summit Lighthouse for their permission that I may show this beautiful Twin Flame illustration in my book. This illustration also decorates the book cover „Soul Mates and Twin Flames – The Spiritual Dimension of Love and Relationships" by Elizabeth Clare Prophet which I recommend for further exploration.

Saint Germain and the Twin Rays

Spiritually speaking, I am pressing the school desk again since my own twin flame experience. I have learned a lot and remembered forgotten things in a very short time; measured in linear time, talking about a few months. Triggered by the realization of my own Soul, the need of awakening became so urgent that I had no other choice but to merge with the truth and absolute love within myself and to give priority to the divine connection over everything external.

One of the first and special memories not very long after my realization that I had met my Twin Flame is the book "The Magic Presence" by Godfré Ray King, in which he tells of encounters with the Ascended Master Saint Germain in the 1930s.

I knew this book for many years and even still have an old edition from 1991, which is no longer available today. In 2015, I myself revised this book for the Saint Germain publishing house in Höhr-Grenzhausen and did the layout, so I could remember particularly well that this book speaks of "Twin Rays".

The special thing about my memory is that in this life I first came in contact with this subject matter through this wonderful book. I remember the taste, the tone, the sound that the descriptions of the twin rays left in my Soul. It was a feeling of knowing that all this is reality on a certain level, it was a feeling of recognition and of very distant longing to want to experience this connection myself. I felt so far away from it that it sounded more like a beautiful unattainable dream.

The book "The Magic Presence" contains so much depth, beauty and truth. Especially through the direct words of Saint Germain and his teachings, I knew inwardly that what was written there was true. In this respect, it has a very deep kinship with my feelings when I read Omnec Onec's autobiography "From Venus I Came" – I just knew intuitively that it was all true and that I was at home in this knowledge.

Against this background, the book "The Magic Presence" together with its twin ray mentions had and has left a trace in me, the path of which my Soul obviously took up decades later and through which it also led my conscious experiences into the experienced reality.

I am including here two quotes from this book that can tell you something about the nature of the twin rays:

> *Rex and Pearl are 'Twin Rays' from the same Divine Flame. The Flame comes forth from the Heart of God, the Great Life Consciousness of the Universe, the Great Central Sun.*
>
> *When You, the 'Mighty I AM Presence,' will to come forth into an Individualized Focus of Conscious Dominion and use the Creative Word 'I AM,' Your first Individual Activity is the formation of a Flame. Then you, the Individualized Focus of the 'Mighty I AM Presence,' begin Your Dynamic Expression of Life.*
>
> *This Activity we term Self-consciousness-meaning the individual who is conscious of his Source and Perfection of Life expressing through himself. Only the Self-conscious Individual has ALL the Attributes and Creative Power of the 'Mighty I AM Presence.' Only He can know who and what He is and express the Fullness of the Creative Power of God whenever He decrees, by the use of the Words 'I AM.'*
>
> *– "The Magic Presence," Book 2 of the Saint Germain Series by Godfré Ray King.*

There is so much more to say about the reality of the twin flames and possibly there will be more revelations about this in other places and in the future – also by me. For this book, I would like to leave it at this and invite you personally to contact me if you would like to learn more about this subject. I feel that because of the intense impact this third initiation has had on me, it is a big part of my life, the dimensions of which I cannot yet survey.

In closing, I share with you here a poem I wrote recently that may give you a sense of what an experience meeting your own Soul can be.

My Love Poem

God has only borrowed me His heart.
It does not belong to me.
Now he has reclaimed it.
He came like a wind –
a shower of light.
A rain full of gold sparks
From above through the chimney pipe
All of a sudden, I did not suspect it before.
THERE it is, the light.
Far, far it pushed open doors and windows from the inside
Like a storm in the living room
He swept through
My heart – all open!
Everything is open – there is no turning back!
There is no more room
The doors and windows no longer close.
Never again.
God came and reclaimed his heart.
I did not understand, I gave it to YOU!
Or did you give me yours first?
And then God came and brought it to me?
It is all light
It is all ONE LOVE
You, God, me – where is the difference?
I do not know anymore.
I AM only LOVE.
I give God his heart back.
It has a place in all of us.
I love you.

Chart No. 3 – Twin Flames – Soul Journey

Twin Flames

- Soul Journey through the Levels of Consciousness -

Image 21: Twin Flames Soul Journey.

One Soul as divine masculine and divine feminine polarity travels through the levels of consciousness. ONE Soul – TWO causal/mental/emotional/ physical bodies. You can download this illustration in color from **venus-spirit.com**.

Epilogue

It seems simple when you look at all the thousands of lives you have lived. Each life looks like a grain of sand and seems so unimportant compared to the eternal existence of the Soul. But when you enter into that grain of sand, that life becomes huge and overwhelming.

Omnec Onec in autobiography part 2 "Angels Don't Cry"

The book is finished. The journey continues.

One station is reached – I leave the package here now. To bring a book into realization is a bit like an incarnation – it is the materialization of something spiritual, which in its individual way leaves a small trace in the huge web of creative threads.

Remembering Omnec Onec's words, which I have prefaced this epilogue, the following thoughts have come to me: When I, as a Soul, am free to simply BE in the formless worlds, I AM everything and ONE, pure consciousness, pure light, pure love. Then when I send a spark of my essence down into a physical embodiment, suddenly everything seems so huge – every thought, every feeling, every physical experience – even every drama, every trauma, every pain. Everything feels so gigantic. And when I return to infinity and have distance, then the whole life as well as the creation of this book was just a small grain of sand on the beach of the ocean of love and grace – and that is as insignificant as it is incredibly valuable and important.

In the end, it is the moments of love that count, every moment of mindfulness, every small kind act of compassion. Everything painful is forgotten, everything unconscious is forgiven, all separation is transformed into oneness.

The journey continues. May it be blissful.

That is what I wish for all of us from the bottom of my heart.

With love

Anja

Appendix: Jo Conrad Interview with Omnec Onec

Image 22: Jo Conrad Interview with Omnec Onec.
Jo Conrad and Omnec Onec – the Legendary Transformation Interview from 1999 (YouTube thumbnail).

This interview by Jo Conrad[15] with Omnec Onec took place in the summer of 1999 in the garden of Seminarhaus Pegasus between the Elbe river and the North Sea. The transcription was originally published in Jo Conrad's book "Ursprünge", 2000, ISBN 978-3933718013.

I sincerely thank Jo Conrad for allowing me to publish his interview with Omnec once again.

15 In the German speaking countries, Jo Conrad is a very well-known and popular truth researcher and author. **https://bewusst.tv/**

Revision of the German text and upload of the original video recording with German subtitles on the YouTube Venus Spirit channel **https://youtube.com/@venus-spirit** by Anja Schäfer.

Direct link to the video: **https://youtu.be/S1fR26Pn3tg**

The Legendary Transformation Interview

Jo: Omnec, our viewers can't imagine that there is life on Venus because science has studied everything and claims that there is no life there. Is this claim true, or is there something science is not telling us? Or can we not detect life there because it is on a different plane?

Omnec: Life on Venus used to be on a physical level like it is now here on Earth. However, that was at least 20 million years ago.

Jo: That was a while ago.

Omnec: Yes. And today our societies and cultures live in a parallel world or dimension to the physical. They are the ancestors of some ancient civilizations on Earth. All races on Earth come from other planets, but that happened at a time before you started writing history.

Jo: Were the Venusians the first visitors or were they just a part of different visitors from space?

Omnec: All human life forms in our solar system came from other galaxies before the Earth became a planet, that is, when the Earth was still a comet that was just becoming a planet. They came to protect this solar system and were chosen to be the higher life form in the universe, because human life forms are the higher life forms. They colonized the oldest four planets in the solar system, namely Mars, Venus, Jupiter and Saturn. These were the four main races that then colonized the Earth and that you know. They originally populated the Earth.

In the present time, the original beings, I do not mean the first visitors, but the descendants of the original races, are living in a parallel dimension with their technologies and their spiritual abilities. We have the ability to manifest a physical body to live and work in the physical world.

Jo: Like you are now?

Omnec: Yes, exactly

Jo: And what about the other planets today? Is there still life there?

Omnec: Yes, but not physically.

Jo: Not physically, but on a different vibrational level, for instance?

Omnec: Yes, that's right. There are even traces and old relics from times past.

Jo: Like the Martian face and the pyramids?

Omnec: Yes, exactly. Some things have already been discovered.

Jo: And there's still life on Mars, just as there is on Venus, at the same level practically?

Omnec: Yes, of course.

Jo: How did you come to be on Earth? How should we imagine that? In a flying saucer or in a UFO?

Omnec: On each of the ancient planets (Mars, Venus, Saturn and Jupiter) there is still an ancient city that exists in both the physical and higher dimensions. It is a hidden city, so to speak.

Jo: On Earth, too?

Omnec: Yes, even on Earth there are these hidden temple complexes in various places. They also serve as interdimensional gateways. But they were hidden a long time ago. On the other planets we have the same facilities and there we can manifest physically. We can also manifest ships there that we use in the physical to travel. We have the ability to travel intergalactically, interdimensionally and in time with our spaceships.

That is how I came to the Earth. After I manifested my physical body on Venus in that particular city, I was taken to a physical ship that brought me to Earth. The first year after my arrival, I lived in Tibet. There I learned to deal with gravity, to speak the language and to use my physical body.

Jo: That is certainly a hard experience to descend from a light, spherical life into a manifested, physical life like ours on Earth.

Omnec: Yes, it is very difficult to get used to a physical body.

Jo: How old were you when you came to Earth? Were you already in your physical body or in the state in which you also lived on Venus? Like as a reincarnation or in a physical body from Venus?

Omnec: According to your chronology, I was seven years old. In our time, however, I was already 130 years old. That is in your time calculation just as long as with us, we live however longer than you and our aging process goes substantially more slowly. And now, according to your calendar, I am about 250 years old.

Yep: But for this age you still look really good.

Omnec: Here on Earth, I look like a 50-year-old woman.

Jo: Why did you come? Do you have a mission, was it voluntary or a mission?

Omnec: All three reasons are correct. First of all, it was the desire of the spiritual hierarchy.

Jo: On Venus itself or somewhere else?

Omnec: The spiritual hierarchy dominates the whole physical universe.

Jo: So everywhere, not just on Venus?

Omnec: Yes, and it has a great deal to do with the destiny of humanity in the physical planes. The Hierarchy is made up of advanced Souls, ascended masters and spiritual beings, many of whom have lived in the physical themselves.

Jo: So ascended masters?

Omnec: Yes, correct.

Jo: Like Jesus?

Omnec: Exactly, Jesus is also an ascended master.
One of my tasks is to remind people of their origins and give them back the information about the Earth and the history that has been lost. This knowledge must be brought back to the people to change the concepts and consciousness. The Earth is now entering a new age, the people on Earth call it "New Age". Therefore, they need to know why they are here and what abilities lie dormant within them.
These are the same teachings that Jesus Christ brought.

Jo: Did you come from Venus alone or are there other Venusians here?

Omnec: No, not just me. There are quite a few.

Yep: So a whole lot of them. But you are the best known, or why do we see you?

Omnec: No, I have been chosen to be known on Earth.

Jo: So there are others who work in other areas?

Omnec: Yes, the others operate differently on Earth.

Jo: Do you have special abilities, like reading my mind or my aura?

Omnec: People have a spiritual closure around their thoughts, a kind of "lock". Thoughts are their private matter, there is a special protection. That is not possible.

Jo: Will you or can't you?

Omnec: I can't. But if people can send thoughts again, then we can receive them. Most on Earth cannot send thoughts, but some can.

Jo: Are there people on Earth with whom you can communicate telepathically?

Omnec: Yes, this is possible with a few who have this ability. In this way I also communicate with beings who are not on Earth.

Jo: On Venus

Omnec: Yes, to get information that I need. It is not channeling, but personal contact with beings I know. Look, a long time ago, people on Earth still had this ability of telepathy and remembered their previous existences and who created them and where they came from. But then, after Atlantis, a genetic manipulation of humanity took place. At that time, an invasion of visitors from another star system took place.

Jo: About ten thousand years ago?

Omnec: Yes, exactly, long before Jesus Christ came.

The genetic manipulation divided people's brains into two halves, thereby taking away their ability to communicate without words, to remember their previous incarnations and where they came from. They were left with only those abilities they needed to physically survive here on Earth. The beings who did this, who came to Earth as invaders, established the Earthly ruling hierarchies, introduced racial segregation, invented the languages and religions, and brought the conflicts into the world. They manipulate and control, and since humans have lost their abilities, it is much easier for them.

All the "secret" knowledge that people on Earth had before the manipulation and all the abilities they possessed were now inaccessible to them. The knowledge was made available only to a special elite, the secret brotherhoods, for study.

The rest of the knowledge is controlled and manipulated information, religious teachings. They have introduced racial segregation and created languages.

Jo: They separated everything from the source.

Omnec: Yes, and they created the conflicts because of these distinctions by races and religions.

Jo: Who were they?

Omnec: Well, I'm not allowed to say what star system they came from. They have since realized what they have done and are now involved in helping Earth and humanity heal through transformation.

Jo: Are they on Earth? Do they visit us or does it happen through reincarnations?

Omnec: Yes, a lot have already incarnated. Many people who were born here feel that they do not belong here, but they cannot explain this feeling with their logical mind.

The Earth and humanity is now going through a transformation process – and everything will be as it was before the genetic manipulation. People will reunite and end all conflicts. That is also the reason why I am here and informing about this.

It starts with changing people's perceptions and views. This is also what I do in my workshops. I teach people to overcome the structured and controlled ideas. When you are born here, you are given your religions, your political views and everything. Everything is taught to you from an early age – nothing is your free will, your free choice.

Your families impart this information to you and even force it on you, believing that all of this is right and best for you. Concepts, views and programs are passed down from generation to generation and it leaves little room for the individual to develop, to be free and to be aware and free of their own real desires.

I try to help people overcome all that has been taken over and reconnect with their inner source. It's important to get clear about what your thoughts, feelings and choices really are. How do you really feel? Finding that out is important in order to let go of the programming that comes from the outside.

That is a big process. People have to go through it individually themselves. I don't have any magic solutions, but I can offer other perspectives and give the keys to overcome old concepts. That's also what my books are about. You don't have to come to my workshops, all the information is in my books.

Jo: So you're saying we all have the fundamental right to be free and make our own decisions?

Omnec: Right. Individual free will is above everything. Every person has the right to choose their own religious path and live the way they want to live. But to really make their own choices, people need the basic knowledge of what being human is and what happened on Earth a long time ago, they need the complete knowledge of human history and nature. If you give them an overview of all the connections, as I do in my workshops, then you give them the opportunity to look at the world, the universe and themselves and their origin from different angles. Not only about physical, human life, but about the essence – about the life force that is inherent in every individual.

Jo: So from that point of view, it is not our fault alone that we are not yet evolved as spiritual beings? It has to do with genetic manipulation?

Omnec: And also with the whole society in which you live here.

Yep: So partly based in manipulation and partly based in your own free will?

Omnec: Well, manipulation runs through all social structures and through one's genetics.

Yep: And it's difficult to overcome all that ..., but it's changing?

Omnec: Yes, because we pull out the manipulations step by step, so to speak, by connecting individually with individuals to show them how to change their views and concepts. Of course, no one HAS to change, people are allowed to decide for themselves what is right for them and what is not.
But once they have the complete information, only then can they really make a free choice. The transformation process then takes its course by itself anyway.

Jo: This is information that we don't get through the mass media.

Omnec: Absolutely right. But even if they had that information, they wouldn't change the schools because it would be too expensive for them.

Jo: It's not intentional for people to get this information?

Omnec: Of course, this is not intentional. Those in power manipulate the energy industries and money.

Any changes threaten their systems and ultimately mean their end, and that's what they want to prevent.

Jo: Power, greed and money.

Omnec: Of course, material things.

Jo: How do you see our development? Are you confident about the future of humanity?

Omnec: Absolutely! You have to illustrate the concepts and connections to people in simple little steps. Just by replacing criticizing and judging with acceptance, you have a completely different way of life, because you are allowing others to make their own free choices. You allow others to decide for themselves what is best for them and their lives and that they are responsible for themselves. Thus, you do not interfere in the affairs of others and do not focus too much on them, but on yourselves. In this way you resolve many conflicts, for you do not create conflicts when you simply say, well, you have your view, you have your reality, you make your own choices. Let them live their lives, because it's their free will.

The greatest problems and conflicts in your world are created when you try to impose your own ideas on others – for this is again exercising control and manipulation.

Jo: Since you came from Venus, have you noticed a change here in terms of human behavior?

Omnec: Yes, certainly! When I wrote my book in the sixties, there was no understanding of other dimensions. There was no way to reach people with this information then. But with the development of the technologies here and your satellite systems, the computers and the communication system, a greater awareness developed. There is now a lot of information available to everyone. This information has changed people and opened the doors to a greater understanding.

Jo: So there are two sides to everything: Information can manipulate, but it can also broaden horizons.

Omnec: Absolutely right. You can distinguish between many more possibilities. You can see the advantages and also recognize the difficulties better.

Jo: Do Venusians have the concept of a God or Creator?

Omnec: Yes, we believe there is only one source – one energy source. Through this energy source, everything exists. This source creates everything that is out of itself in never-ending cycles. In this way, the source exists forever.

Jo: Are we a part of it or is it high above us?

Omnec: This source, this creative energy or creator is present in every living thing. It exists through all living things.

Jo: That sounds somewhat different from what we know from the Bible. There, we are given a different image of God.

Omnec: True. Imagine a centrifuge that is spinning fast. Now throw stones, sand and water into it. The heavier material will collect on the outside – this area corresponds to the physical dimension. The further you look inside, the lighter the material. In the center itself, you have pure energy. There is the center of creation – the source of energy.

All other worlds or dimensions go down to the physical plane, which corresponds to the material world in which we are living here right now. Of course, as a human being, you must have a physical body in order to have experiences here. The Soul, this little spark of the creative source, has the ability to envelop itself with a body in each dimension – a body that has the same energy as the corresponding dimension. In these other dimensions the Soul stays when it is not in the physical.

Jo: So not only do we have a physical body, but parts of us are also in the higher dimensions closer to the center of creation?

Omnec: Right. Your body is just a vehicle in which you live and with which you have your experiences in this world. You can communicate and move around in this world with it. But the essence of your being is the Soul. And when your body stops functioning, the Soul lives on in the other dimensions. When it chooses to come back to the physical world, it makes that choice in terms of the experiences it wishes to have. This is what I teach in my workshops. I explain the whole concept of creation and your connection with everything and that you too are an infinite, creative source of life.

Jo: And love is the key to everything?

Omnec: Yes. True love is the energy of the Creator, and it flows through everything that lives. Without love, there would be nothing.

I am talking about unconditional love, not the conditional love that exists in your societies. Unconditional love means: I love you because you ARE. For no other reason.

Jo: So not only if you love me too.

Omnec: ... or if you do what I want.

Yep: So there are some things here on Earth that are different than on Venus.

Do you have sex on Venus or is it a purely physical affair?

Omnec: When we still had a physical society on Venus, of course. Now that we no longer have physical bodies there, we still know sensations. We have astral bodies and we have the force of attraction. We can exchange energy with each other. It's almost the same feeling as sex in the physical, only more intense. After all, it is the same energy and we can feel the exchange of energies.

Jo: I think sexuality is a big problem with people who are looking for spiritual development.

Omnec: Well, I think that sexuality is a function of the physical body and basically very healthy and useful. In your societies, sexuality has often been abused and misunderstood, and there are many difficulties and morals associated with that. There are many problems due to repression and lack of understanding of what sexuality actually is.

You should not build a relationship on sexual attraction. A relationship should be a true connection between all human levels – emotional, mental and spiritual – and sexuality should be a part of that special connection and complement it. But if you build a relationship on sexuality, it is naturally not very stable.

Jo: We have a development at the moment that a lot of people are talking about their sex life in the big media. Again, there seems to be two sides to this: On the one hand, while it's mainly about physical sexuality and not about true love, on the other hand, it makes us more tolerant of different sexual behaviors among people. Do you see it the same way?

Omnec: Yes, there are all kinds of forms of sex therapy, a lot of useful information, but there is also still so much repression that runs very deep and all of that repression has led to so much abuse in this area. It's only because of this repression and lack of honest expression that you have also developed criminal tendencies and sexual abuse.

I am also referring to exaggeration. The key to a harmonious life is balance.

When one becomes fanatical, even health fanatical, not allowing oneself or others a drop of alcohol, no sexuality – even then one suppresses natural tendencies. One tries to achieve a perfection that is not realistic in this world.

In this world, you are a physical being. This also means that you should give yourself permission to be a part of the so-called negative and positive, and equally strive for balance and have understanding of your limitations.

In exaggeration lies the real danger. To be fanatical in one way is also to be imbalanced. Everyone has to find their own balance, and that is something I cannot tell anyone – everyone has to find that out for themselves.

Again, judging and criticizing plays an important role. If you eat a perfect vegetarian diet, don't smoke, don't drink, and so on, and then look at others and think they are wrong for doing all these things, then you are criticizing again and are not balanced in that way. Again, it's not an expression of letting others live and be as they choose. This is what I mean by acceptance and balance.

Jo: You mean we should not judge others and their lives, but accept them as they are?

Omnec: Exactly. We are all alive. Humans live, plants live, and animals live – all living things contain the same essence and serve a purpose. It is only your individual choice to choose how you want to live and no one has the right to decide but yourself.

Jo: Another topic – technology on Venus: Do you have technologies there, like we know from science fiction movies? For example, small communication systems, beaming – can you tell something about that?

Omnec: Yes, we have all these capabilities. We have big spaceships that are like cities, we have small ships that can make themselves visible and invisible because they can change between dimensions. They can change their frequency, their vibration. Yes, what you know as science fiction, we have all that. But for us, it's all natural. Great technology evolves along with advanced consciousness, because that technology works in harmony with creation. It does not deplete, consume or destroy, it works in harmony with the universe. It is a vibrational, magnetic energy that we harness. It is related to the progress of our thought process – to our consciousness.

Jo: Are these technologies also available to us when we are more spiritually advanced?

Omnec: When you understand the energy that flows through your body from the other dimensions – it flows through us 24 hours continuously and most people don't know that and so they just use up their energy. Wherever you put your attention, that's where you send your energy. If you focus your energy on a negative aspect of life or on fears, for example, if you are afraid of war, then you are reinforcing those very things with your energy. That's exactly what I show people – I show them how to consciously align their energy to bless those particular areas or issues. In this way, people can send out a unified force and stop what they really don't want to have.

I teach people in my workshops how to feel the life energy that is constantly flowing through their bodies and I also show them where in the body these energy points are, where the energies from the other dimensions flow in and out.

Jo: You mean the chakras?

Omnec: Yes, exactly. And I also explain the effects of the other dimensions on the human body.

Jo: All of these are very old teachings, aren't they?

Omnec: Yes, that's right, they are even older than the Earth.

Jo: So you're not the first to share this knowledge like this?

Omnec: No, but what I do is to give a simple explanation of all this that is not complicated. I always try to explain everything in simple terms so that everyone can understand it and directly relate it to themselves and their lives. It's important that the teachings don't seem so strange and detached, so that you can't understand anything and have no idea what I'm talking about.

Jo: But you don't use technologies from Venus to impress people or to prove to them that you are from Venus?

Omnec: No, I don't think that's necessary. I don't like it either, because this would be a kind of showmanship, I don't need that. It's sensational enough what people learn about themselves through this information.

Jo: That means people just have to believe what you say?

Omnec: What matters is that people believe in themselves. It doesn't matter whether they believe me or not. My knowledge speaks for itself.

Jo: Yes, I think it does. But I'm sure some people don't want to believe it.

Omnec: I have a faster heartbeat than Earth people, I carry my children longer than Earth women, I make my own calcium, which is good for renewing my teeth, for example.

Jo: Can we humans do that too, or is it a special gift?

Omnec: You know, you have a lot of abilities in truth, but medicine and the media have convinced you that this and that is bad for your health, that at 65 you're old news and you have to retire and that you don't function well anymore and so on, and people believe that and that's why they become that way. I don't believe any of that, I'm around 50 years old now and I enjoy my life like a twenty year old, I have a lot of energy, I can also have a glass of wine or smoke a cigarette and control that. I know that these things do no harm to my body.

Jo: What can you say about cancer or AIDS? Where do these diseases come from, and will we beat them?

Omnec: Some diseases, I think, are intentionally created by your governments to eliminate so-called "undesirable societies." And I think that these intentions are thrown back to their creators – as a kind of punishment. When they start using their technologies to improve what the Creator has created, it always means the downfall of civilization.

Jo: The genetic modifications, you mean? You want to improve something that is already perfect.

Omnec: Exactly. They don't see that creation is already perfect. They think what doesn't seem to be perfect needs to be improved. I see it differently – I see that all imperfections are unique qualities that we should value.

Jo: So our view of disease tends to be misconceptions or misunderstandings?

Omnec: Well, some diseases are created by the media. They publish books and say this causes cancer, that causes cancer. Then when people take this information into their belief systems, they create these diseases in their bodies out of their fear.

Jo: So it's the thoughts that manifest the diseases?

Omnec: Yes, if people really believe it, they create it. That's what I'm talking about: Whatever you believe, whatever you incorporate into your thought system, and if you really accept it as truth, then it becomes a part of you. On the other hand, if you know that it's not true, that you don't recognize something as a danger to you – of course, you shouldn't overdo it in any way, but consume only enough of everything that it's still enjoyment – then none of that creates a disease in you. Of course, you can get sick if you overdo it and harm your body.

I think spreading fear-mongering information is a way to keep the chemical companies and doctors alive in your system.

Jo: This is driven by greed for power and money.

Omnec: Everything always comes back to the same thing, right. In reality, people have the ability to live much longer.

Jo: So we don't have to die at all when we reach an age of about 75?

Omnec: No, I don't think so.

Jo: So all you have to do is change your thinking?

Omnec: Yes. I teach people not only to believe but also to know. There is a difference between belief and knowledge.

Jo: You say that fear is part of these diseases.

Omnec: Fear is the most powerful tool they have in your societies to control people. It is used in your churches, in your schools, in your families. Fear is the key to control everything that happens. People can overcome fear by realizing that their physical bodies may die, but that the essence remains. Death is only a transition from one form of existence to another. In the higher dimensions, you then learn what you cannot grasp here.

Jo: So afterwards you come back to learn the things you didn't learn? Does reincarnation exist?

Omnec: It's your free choice.

Jo: So you voluntarily say to yourself something like: Oh, I guess I screwed that up – now I'm coming back – or how does that work?

Omnec: You're making attachments here – and then there's the fear of death. You feel like you haven't completed something. Or you messed up in a relationship and you didn't have a chance to fix it or take responsibility for it anymore, then you feel out of yourself that you want to go back. So sometimes you feel yourself going back out of a sense that something is missing, that you haven't taken responsibility for your actions yet.

Jo: You say that we are facing something like a transformation.

Omnec: Correct. This transformation began in 1993, when we activated the ancient hidden temples on Earth. These temples also serve as gateways to the other, higher dimensions. The spiritual hierarchy in the higher dimensions then started sending energy to Earth. They have instructed nature – the birds, the insects, the natural beings, the elements – to change their frequency through their sounds. The sounds of nature are useful and healing for the planet. Many spiritual groups were formed and they started regular meditation in different places of the world. The whole process is guided and carried out by spiritual sources.

In addition, large spaceships have positioned themselves in various locations around the Earth. They, too, are sending energy to Earth. All in all, it is a cooperative interaction of millions of beings from different places in the galaxy and from different dimensions to return the Earth and the people to their natural state.

For this purpose, a new chakra system is created in people. This helps to synchronize the two hemispheres of the brain so that they function together again. Abilities like intuition, insight, memories of your former existences and of your true self will return. You will again intuitively know what and whom to believe – in other words – you will again know who is deceiving you and who is honest. All these natural abilities will return to you.

The next generation will be born with all these abilities genetically intact. But we who already live here get this artificial support system from the other dimensions that helps the Earth and us to go through the transformation process.

This means that the frequency of the Earth will change and move to a higher vibration. There will be a point when conventional technology will no longer work here. All this is not happening overnight – it has been going on since 1993 and is a gradual process, because we do not want to harm human bodies.

There may already be problems even with the millennium change to the year 2000 because of the changeover of computers. People must see that they cannot really rely on the technology here. In the future, it will no longer work in the known way.

The political systems are already wobbling. They are based on corruption and this will come to light more and more. The political systems will collapse through their own unjust actions and the people here will become more and more aware of it. They will realize it and lose more and more of their trust. All of this will fall apart. When money loses its value, people will learn to look to themselves and survive on their own. The people ARE the power. You have all these industries and companies that have a monopoly on everything. But the people who work for them are the ones who, through their energy, keep the functionality of each sector alive. If they leave and take their labor and energy with them, then those who own these companies can no longer function without the workers. Eventually, people will realize this and understand that it is not they who need the industries, but the industries who need the people.

Jo: What awaits us is not the end of the world, but a change, a transformation.

Omnec: Yes, exactly. But people will survive because they have acquired all the knowledge they need through their occupations. They know how to build houses and how to make and produce everything they need to survive. People will connect and network and you will form a new society. Many will also die – there will also be suicides of industrialists and bankers and others when they realize that what they have worked for all their lives and all their money are worth nothing. Rather, the people who survive will be those who never had much anyway.

Jo: Are the electromagnetic waves emitted by our microwaves and cell phones harmful to us? Do they interfere with our connection with the higher dimensions?

Omnec: They are harmful, but even these things will eventually stop working.

Look, new technology is being introduced here. Once the conventional technology no longer works and the transformation process is complete. There will certainly be a lot of destruction and panic among people. That is also the reason why I am here and informing about it. People will pass on this information and then there will be enough who will not panic and help the frightened people. There will be places and centers where people can meet, feel safe and get information. Also, people can find information about the transformation on the Internet and keep up to date. There will be many meditations and meditation groups, and networks for contacts. When the transformation is complete, new technologies will be introduced and you will live in a different way than before.

Jo: What new technology?

Omnec: Free energy: magnetic power, solar power, anything that works in harmony with nature.

Jo: No electronics? Like photonic energy?

Omnec: You will have magnetic vibrational energy. We will also share information about crystals and their powers that were known in ancient times, there will be healing possibilities that come from within your own self.

You know, there is a lot of free energy on Earth and devices already exist. My first publisher has published many books and videos about free energy. There are lists, books and videos on this subject and many people have already made inventions, but they cannot be used because the energy industry prevents it.

Jo: So it's all there already and at some point it's going to be time where we get to use these techniques?

Omnec: Yes, there are many people just waiting to make their devices available to the public.

Jo: These are encouraging prospects.

Omnec: Yes, it will become a better world, but the transition period will be difficult. There will be a lot of panic among people who can't accept and go along with this transformation. Mostly because they are not informed and don't know what is going on. Some hurt each other out of fear and panic, but their Souls will return in new bodies, more comfortable with the new world. After all, you can't kill the Soul.

Jo: Are the Venusians helping us with this process? You are here now – are there others?

Omnec: Yes, the Venusians are here, also Sirians and many others. There are many galaxies and beings involved in this cooperative process – including the Pleiadians. Some of them don't look human. Of course, there are also the beings from the other dimensions. What I say here, you will find in all prophecies from all countries.

Jo: What's with the little horrors and kidnappings?

Omnec: These are negative beings.

Jo: So this is real?

Omnec: Governments have made deals with them for technology and given them permission to kidnap people in return.

Jo: So Roswell was real?

Omnec: Yes. And the governments are doing business with these beings. When we reactivated the hidden temples around the Earth, we also put a protective field around the Earth to prevent that from happening any further.

Jo: That sounds good. Omnec, do you have anything else important to tell the people of Earth?

Omnec: Imagination is the key to creating reality. Everything that exists was previously in your imagination. If you do not set limits to it, then what you can imagine can exist.

Jo: That sounds good. Omnec, thank you for the interview, have a great time here on Earth.

Omnec: You're very welcome. I hope you also learned a lot about yourself and your transformation.

Image Directory

Publisher's Recommendations

Venus Pearls

From Venus I Came

Omnec Onec

Omnec Onec was born on the astral level of the planet Venus and came to Earth with her own physical body in 1955. She tells about the history, spirituality and culture of the Venusians, who once were a physical society and who have lived on the astral plane for a long time. Omnec tells about her first years of life on the astral Venus, explains why and how she came to Earth and what mission she has to fulfill here. This book is a unique document of its kind about the fabulous world of the astral. Being a sister planet to Earth, Venus has already gone through a similar process of transformation into a higher frequency plane as the Earth and its inhabitants are currently going through.

The history of Venus, delivered through Omnec Onec, along with its spiritual teachings, are a gift of pure love and show how the transformation into an expanded consciousness can be mastered in accordance with the universal laws of the Supreme Deity. This book is the authorized re-publication of the original version as written by Omnec Onec in the 1960s and first published in the USA in 1991 under the title UFO – From Venus I Came.

New Release 2023, DISCUS Publishing

ISBN: 978-3-910804-09-8

Angels Don't Cry
Omnec Onec
Angels Don't Cry is the stunning sequel to Omnec Onec's autobiography "**From Venus I Came**". This book is about the earthly life of the Venusian. Difficult family circumstances, constant changes of location and a spiritually unawakened environment presented very challenging conditions for the conscious child from Venus. The telepathic and sometimes physical contact with her friends and relatives from Venus as well as the awareness of her mission gave Omnec the strength to endure this life and to master it in love. Slowly, Omnec's way to the public was paved and the fulfillment of her mission as an Ambassador of Venus took hold with the first publication of her life story by Lt. Col. Ret. Wendelle C. Stevens in 1991.
New Release 2023, DISCUS Publishing
ISBN: 978-3-910804-10-4

Handbook of Venusian Spirituality
Omnec Onec
Essence of Spiritual Teachings
The truth is always simple. Practical and current, Omnec writes about the essence of creation, Soul, and life. This volume contains the essential message of the Venusian and gives practical keys for the expansion of consciousness.
Publisher's Note: This Handbook has never been published in English in this version as a separate book before. Parts of it are included in the Venusian Trilogy.
New Release 2023, DISCUS Publishing
ISBN: 978-3-910804-11-1

The Venusian Trilogy
Contents:
"From Venus I Came" - Autobiography part 1
A classic in spiritual literature: In her autobiography, Omnec Onec portrays her life on the astral level of Venus and teaches timeless wisdom. She speaks about the adventure of how and why she decided to manifest a physical body, and about her journey to Earth in 1955. This book was first published by the US Col. Wendelle C. Stevens in 1991.
"Angels Don't Cry" - Autobiography part 2
In the continuation of her autobiography, Omnec tells her experiences on Earth.
"My Message" - Essence of spiritual teachings. Omnec writes about the essence of creation, Soul, and life. This part also contains a chapter about the evolution of Souls on Earth.
Note: This edition contains all of Omnec's three books and was compiled and in some parts revised by her supporter and deceased previous publisher Kouki Wohlwend in 2012.
544 pages with colored pictures
ISBN: 978-3-9523815-2-6

Simply Wisdom and Love - Venusian Spirituality
Omnec Onec and Anja Schäfer
The world as we know it is changing rapidly, the Transformation Process of the Earth is in progress. The current world system, in which a few powerful people control and manipulate others, is coming to an end. The Earth is ascending to a higher frequency. Thanks to courageous messengers such as

Omnec Onec, we are reminded of what we have long forgotten: that our ancestors came from other star systems and galaxies. Our existence is not limited to the physical life we live. We are all Souls and universal beings, created by a loving Creator.
Contents: The Unknown History of our Solar System and the ongoing Transformation of the Earth from Venusian perspective · "The True Story of Christ" · "A Venusian Letter" · Transcripts of Omnec's public appearances with Q&A · Project Omnec's Oasis – a Place to live in Harmony with the Universe
Loving, wise, inspiring. This book is a light focus for the expansion of consciousness and gives a deep insight into the teachings of the Venusians.
DISCUS Publishing, 2016
ISBN: 978-3-9817441-0-1

Venus and I
Anja Schäfer
My Journey of Coming to Remembrance of my Soul Mission
— 25 years with Omnec Onec —
A Story about Initiations, the Transformation of the Earth, and Love
"This book describes the author's spiritual awakening process. Her refreshing and witty way of writing made me feel like I was along on her journey."
Axel
Contents: Venus Ambassadors, Omnec Onec, Dr. Raymond Keller "Cosmic Ray", Phaistos Disc, Atlantis, Cyclic Time – Linear Time, Venus-Germany-Connection, Transformation and Future of the Earth, Ascension, Awakening, Artificial Timeline (2D) and Natural Timeline (5D), Spiritual Practices, Levels of Consciousness, Journey of Soul, Twin Flames, Unconditional Love, Jo Conrad Interview with Omnec Onec.
"I am certain today that I have incarnated as one of the souls to break down encrusted structures and to help both myself and

people to allow true, divine love to rise and to embody. We are here to help Mother Earth to ascend to a higher vibrational frequency and to end the age of darkness and ignorance."
Anja Schäfer – *venus-spirit.com*
New Release 2023, DISCUS Publishing
ISBN: 978-3-910804-02-9

Venus Historian Dr. Raymond Keller

Dr. Raymond Andrew Keller aka "Cosmic Ray" is the Historian of the Venusians, contactee, UFO researcher, author and retired Doctor of History. Ray's VENUS RISING book series explores numerous facets of Venus. Well documented and based on personal research and years of experience, Ray's books reveal amazing connections from the perspectives of history, mythology, theosophy, space exploration, ufology, contactees, Venusians, spirituality, and current events.

Venus Rising – A Concise History of the Second Planet, 2016
The Final Countdown: Rockets to Venus, 2018
Cosmic Rays Excellent Venus Adventure, 2018
The Vast Venus Conspiracy, 2021

Lady Columba Venus Revelations, 2021
Flying Saucers and the Venus Legacy, 2022
From Venus They Come, 2022
Book 1 to 7 published by Headline Books, WV, USA *https://headlinebooks.com/* in cooperation with Dr. Keller.
More about Cosmic Ray: https://venus-spirit.com/ray

The Gospels of Thomas and Mary Magdalene

Dr. Raymond Keller

This Gospel of Thomas, inclusive of the Gospel of Mary Magdalene, was found at the Nag Hammadi site in the Egyptian desert in December of 1945 along with some other books collectively called the "Nag Hammadi Library." These texts were very fragmented with age and in a state of advanced decay. The original parchments now rest in the Coptic Museum in Cairo. They have been thought to have been written and dated from 100-245 A.D., according to some sources.

Until today these sacred texts have only been able to be partially interpreted by scholars because no complete record of these texts has ever been found. That these texts are even real is debated by many. It is possible, but doubtful, that these texts are in their complete form anywhere in the world, not even in the library beneath the Vatican. Even if these texts were there, they could not be as complete or as accurate as this version for this edition is a supernatural gift to the faithful through the Hierarchy of Light.

2022, DISCUS Publishing
ISBN: 978-3-9817441-9-4

CDs from Omnec Onec

In collaboration with the music producer Wulf Wemmje, Omnec Onec created these three beautiful CDs under Venusian inspiration.

Soul Journey
Guided Meditation with various music compositions corresponding to the levels of consciousness. Mantras and visualizations support the experience of the different dimensions from the physical through the astral, the causal, and the etheric dimension to the God planes. *"The Soul Travel technique enables you to leave the physical body withouth the connection of the silver chord. You travel with light and sound and have access to any dimension you wish, where you can gain knowledge or make an experience for the benefit of Soul while still existing in the physical."*

My Mission on Earth
Omnec tells the story of her origin and shares universal knowledge
Listen to Omnec's fascinating voice, embedded in sound spheres and Venusian inspired music, how she describes in her own words the connection of Venus to the history of the Earth and the purpose and goal of her adventurous transfer from the astral plane to the physical Earth.

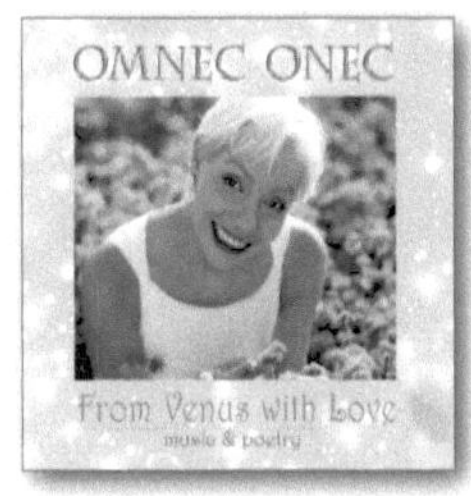

From Venus with Love

Omnec speaks and sings about love with spherical background music. "Love in the physical realm is one of the most powerful emotions, that is expressed in unlimited ways. Love can overwhelm the senses, or love can be subtle. Love is different for each of us. Love can be used to create, or love can destroy. Love can be used to manipulate and control, or love can be given freely. Love can make you a prisoner, and love can make you free. Once you have experienced love in all forms, then you get to know unconditional love. Venus Love is unconditional love." (Omnec Onec, Introduction CD "From Venus with Love")

These CDs are available physically and as downloads in our **Venus Spirit Online-Shop https://venus-spirit.com.** Here, you can also enjoy audio samples.

Contact

Anja Schäfer

Venus Spirit Website: *https://venus-spirit.com*
Omnec Onec Website: *https://omnec-onec.com*

Venus Spirit YouTube Channel:
https://www.youtube.com/@venus-spirit

Please subscribe to our **Venus Spirit Newsletter**.

Let's connect more and more with each other and create an amazing new Earth together!

May the Universal Love and Blessings Be

Anja ♥

www.ingramcontent.com/pod-product-compliance
Ingram Content Group UK Ltd.
Pitfield, Milton Keynes, MK11 3LW, UK
UKHW041842190726
13854UKWH00002B/673